Sentence Combination

WRITING, COMBINING, AND EDITING STANDARD ENGLISH SENTENCES

Book II

SECOND EDITION

Lynn E. Henrichsen • *Alice C. Pack*

BRIGHAM YOUNG UNIVERSITY, HAWAII CAMPUS

Heinle & Heinle Publishers
A Division of Wadsworth, Inc.
Boston, Massachusetts 02116

Publisher: Stanley J. Galek
Editorial Director: David C. Lee
Project Editor: Ros Herion Freese
Editorial Production Manager: Elizabeth Holthaus
Production Editor: Kristin Thalheimer
Manufacturing Coordinator: Lisa McLaughlin
Interior Design: Ros Herion Freese
Cover Design: Robert Pehlke

*Sentence Combination: Writing, Combining, and Editing
Standard English Sentences*

Heinle & Heinle Publishers is a division of Wadsworth, Inc.

Manufactured in the United States of America.

Library of Congress Cataloging-in-Publication Data

Henrichsen, Lynn E.
    Writing, combining, and editing standard English sentences / Lynn
E. Henrichsen, Alice C. Pack. -- 2nd ed.
        p.   cm.
    Rev. ed. of: Writing and combining standard English sentences /
Alice C. Pack, Lynn E. Henrichsen. 1980-
    Contents: bk. 1. Sentence construction -- bk. 2. Sentence
combination.
    ISBN 0-8384-3015-5. -- ISBN 0-8384-3017-1
    1. English language--Textbooks for foreign speakers. 2. English
language--Sentences. 3. English language--Rhetoric. I. Pack,
Alice C. II. Pack, Alice C. Writing and combining standard English
sentences. III. Title.
PE1128.H432 1992   91-44906
428.2'4--dc20   CIP

ISBN 0-8384-3017-1

10 9 8 7 6 5 4 3 2 1

Contents

Why This Book Uses "New" Grammar Terms

In *Sentence Combination* (and *Sentence Construction*) you will occasionally encounter new terms like *aux-word, shifter, dummy subject,* and *d-t-n form,* which may be unfamiliar to you. There are two reasons why these terms are used:

- **Of the many varying grammar terms, those used in this book have proven most helpful to students.**

Even among traditional grammar experts, there is considerable variation regarding terminology. For example, what *Sentence Construction* calls a "dummy subject" is called many different things in other grammar books—"anticipatory *it* as subject," "impersonal *it,*" or "*it* expletive." What *Sentence Combination* calls a "half-sentence" various other books call a "participial phrase," "nonfinite verb clause in which the verb is an *-ing* participle," "*-ing* clause without a subject," "absolute construction," "nominative absolute," or "disjunctive dependent clause." In preparing *Sentence Construction* and *Sentence Combination,* a choice had to be made regarding the use of these terms.*

The principle guiding this choice was to use the clearest, most descriptive terms possible. Sometimes this meant using traditional terms. In other cases, however, traditional terms were not satisfactory. For instance, the term *present participle* is not used in the books because it is misleading. (The *-ing form* is actually timeless and can be used in both present and past tenses.) In other cases, however, traditional grammar terms have been employed, or new, compromise terms have been coined.

- **The new terms are part of the process of helping you gain a new understanding of how modern, written English actually works.**

The use of these new terms involves more than just putting new labels on the same old grammar points. As you study the explanations in *Sentence Construction* and *Sentence Combination,* you will realize that there are additional differences in the ways they explain the system of English.

For instance, many of the explanations employ a grammar system called "sector analysis," which was specially designed for teaching the mechanics of modern, written English. Others use a tense-aspect approach to explain English verbs and time relationships. These nontraditional approaches have been adopted because they have proven more effective than traditional Latin-based or nonpedagogically oriented approaches to teaching students how written English works. One of the books' great strengths is that, besides being more easily taught and learned, the new perspective on English grammar that they present reflects the actual workings of modern, written English more accurately.

For example, in Latin-based grammar the traditional approach to parts of speech barely recognizes the auxiliary (calling it a "helping verb") and relegates it to a secondary, supporting role. Nevertheless, as English has evolved in recent centuries, the auxiliary has taken on a variety of powerful and pervasive functions,

---

*Many explanations do mention alternate terms, and Appendix C lists additional "translations" of grammar terms.

becoming all but indispensable for question and negative formation, serving to mark emphasis in written English, and frequently functioning as a substitute for the entire predicate. These are roles that the auxiliary did not play in modern English's ancestral forms, nor in most other languages, and certainly not in Latin, the language on which traditional grammar is based. Sector analysis, however, gives the "aux-word" the emphasis that its importance in modern English merits.

Likewise, the infinitive form and the subjunctive mood of verbs, which are so important in Latin and many Romance languages, simply do not have parallel functions in modern English. While not ignoring these grammar points (the different uses of infinitives are treated in Chapters 5, 7, and 13, and the subjunctive is mentioned in Chapter 13), the grammar explanations in *Sentence Construction* and *Sentence Combination* recognize these differences and treat these grammar points accordingly.

If you are accustomed to some version of traditional, Latin-based grammar, you may find the nontraditional grammar explanations and terminology used in *Sentence Construction* and *Sentence Combination* somewhat different at first. Nevertheless, experience using these books with thousands of students for over ten years has demonstrated that if you accept these new approaches and learn to understand and use them, they will help you.

To the Student

The purpose of this book is to teach you how to produce complex English sentences of the types normally used in edited, academic writing. It provides explicit instruction focusing on a variety of methods for combining and transforming simple basic sentences into longer, more complex ones. As you master these processes, your writing will naturally demonstrate greater variety and maturity. Furthermore, the conscious knowledge of these combining processes will allow you to monitor and edit your writing by (1) checking to make certain that your complex sentences are put together correctly, and (2) experimenting with different combining methods to see which one or ones work best in a particular sentence.

A basic assumption underlying *Sentence Combination* is that students who use it can already write virtually error-free basic sentences. Otherwise, they will end up combining incorrect sentences, which is a lot like building a house with crooked, defective lumber. The results will not be satisfactory.

If you still have trouble with English verb forms and tenses, articles, nouns and pronouns, word forms, and/or basic sentence structure, you need to start with *Sentence Construction,* Book I in this series. It focuses on selected "trouble spots"—areas where most non-native users of standard English experience persistent difficulty when they write—and will help you overcome these difficulties and produce correct basic sentences.

As noted in the preceding section, both books employ a system called sector analysis, a grammar specially designed for teaching the mechanics of modern, written English. They also use a tense-aspect approach to explain English verbs and time relationships. Thousands of students from various linguistic, cultural, and educational backgrounds have used these approaches and these books with great success. They now write English with fewer errors and greater confidence. You can too.

To the Teacher

The primary purpose of this volume and its companion, *Sentence Construction,* is to teach intermediate and advanced students of English as a second language (and standard English as a second dialect) to write grammatically correct, expository prose of the type generally expected in academic situations. Besides helping them produce correct written English to start with, the conscious knowledge of grammar rules which students gain from the explanations and exercises in these books will also help them as they proofread, "monitor," and edit their writing.

Sentence Construction, Book I in the series, teaches students to write correct basic sentences. Explanations and practice exercises help learners overcome problems in areas which have proven to be persistently difficult for most non-native users of standard English. These areas include derivational and inflectional endings of content words, articles and their use with various types of nouns, pronoun usage, basic sentence structure, the complex auxiliary and verb system of modern English, and the different time relationships this system indicates.

This book, *Sentence Combination,* teaches numerous techniques that students can employ to build, transform, and combine their simple sentences in order to produce complexity, variety, and maturity in their writing. *Sentence Combination* builds on the foundation established in *Sentence Construction* and frequently refers to it. Therefore, to avoid confusion, the chapters in *Sentence Construction* are numbered 1 through 7, and the chapters in this book begin with number 8.

In *Sentence Construction,* student production is limited to writing and editing correct basic sentences. *Sentence Combination* teaches numerous sentence-building, transforming, and combining techniques that students can employ to produce complexity, variety, and maturity in their writing.

Explanatory sections are kept as brief, nontechnical, and student-oriented as possible. They are broken down into small, sequenced increments and accompanied by numerous examples as well as explanatory charts and diagrams.

As noted above, many of the explanations are nontraditional. Some are based on sector analysis, a special pedagogical grammar of written English designed by Professor Robert L. Allen of Teachers College, Columbia University. Those dealing with verbs and time rely heavily on the tense-aspect system elaborated by Professor William E. Bull of the University of California at Los Angeles. These new approaches have been adopted because they have proven more effective than traditional Latin-based or nonpedagogically oriented approaches to teaching students how written English works.

When it has proven useful by virtue of being more descriptive or clear, new terminology has also been adopted. In other cases, however, traditional grammar terms have been employed, or new, compromise terms have been coined. The guiding principle in all these decisions has been to use what is most helpful in making English grammar clear to students.

The primary pedagogical principle behind the design of these books is that students learn by doing. In other words, they learn to write by writing, and they gain more from practice writing exercises than they do from a teacher's explanatory presentations. Nevertheless, clear guidance from a teacher can make students' practice more effective. Therefore, in *Sentence Construction* and *Sentence Combination,* brief, focused explanations are followed by generously long sets of assignments. Grammar explanations are limited to what is pedagogically useful with the expectation that most learning will take place as students work through assignments. Teachers are urged to bear this principle in mind and keep their explanatory presentations brief, simple, and to the point, even if they tend to be somewhat general. Students can always go back and read the explanations in the book if they need detailed guidance. In fact, they will probably learn better and remember longer the things they learn when looking for the answer to a question. For this reason, during and after the time when students are working on the practice exercises in class, the teacher should allow time for the discussion of details and the answering of questions from students.

Additional guidelines and suggestions for using *Sentence Construction* and *Sentence Combination* are provided in the teacher's manual (available from the publisher). This guide also provides diagnostic material, an answer key for the exercises, and an achievement test for each chapter in *Sentence Construction.*

Preface to the Second Edition

Those familiar with the first edition of *Sentence Construction* and *Sentence Combination* will notice a number of improvements in this second edition. These revisions reflect over ten years of experience in using the first edition with students from a wide variety of linguistic, cultural, and educational backgrounds. Overall, the modifications have the effect of eliminating the first edition's weaknesses while maintaining its strengths and building new ones. The books are now not only easier to use but more effective in helping students master the challenges of writing, combining, and editing English sentences.

A number of changes reflect recognition of the fact that writing is a process that involves writing and rewriting. Changes in this new edition encourage students to follow the same "monitoring," proofreading, and editing processes that good writers typically go through. In this regard, the need for a conscious understanding of grammar rules, which *Sentence Construction* and *Sentence Combination* have always developed, gains a new rationale as a tool for evaluating what one has already written. Additional, new features, such as the display of sample mistakes (actual student errors in most cases) at the beginning of each chapter and the proofreading exercises at the end of the first six chapters, emphasize and encourage these rewriting processes.

Another major improvement is the provision of a teacher's manual, which provides guidance for using *Sentence Construction* and *Sentence Combination*, a more detailed rationale for the approach they employ, an answer key for the exercises, and achievement tests for each chapter in *Sentence Construction*.

Although explanations in both books continue to rely on sector analysis and the tense-aspect system of English auxiliaries and verbs, many of them have been rewritten to improve their clarity and their completeness. In addition, a few new sections have been added, such as the one that explains the use of verb tenses to show real and unreal conditions.

The exercises as a whole maintain the continuous-context feature that makes them more natural and realistic. Nevertheless, many old exercises have been modified and a number of new ones created. Some of these new exercises support the explanations in the newly added sections, but most either replace old exercises that were outdated or less effective or provide additional practice in areas in which students experience greater difficulty and thus need extra practice. In several cases, student response procedures have also been modified to make the exercises easier to use and/or correct.

Another major difference between the first and second editions is the location of the chapter on modifiers, which is now in Book II, *Sentence Combination*. This change recognizes the fact that many of the procedures taught in this chapter involve sentence combining. It also allows Book I, *Sentence Construction*, to end at a more natural point (the sentence). Furthermore, it evens out the length of the two books, making them more suitable for many semester/quarter calendars.

The single, most important reason behind all these changes was to make the books more effective in the classroom. Suggestions from users of *Sentence Construction* and *Sentence Combination* regarding additional improvements are always welcome and should be sent to Dr. Lynn E. Henrichsen [Language, Literature and Communications Division, Brigham Young University–Hawaii, Laie, HI 96762-1294 (USA)].

L.E.H.

Acknowledgments

We are deeply indebted to the numerous friends, colleagues, and students who have worked with us during the production and revision of *Sentence Construction* and *Sentence Combination*. Without their helpful advice and enthusiastic encouragement, the dream which these books represent would never have become a reality.

First of all, we want to thank the many students in the English Language Institute at Brigham Young University–Hawaii and at the Universidad Autónoma de Chihuahua who used trial versions of the materials. They represent over 50 different mother tongues, and their reactions and suggestions have proven extremely useful.

Over the years, many teachers have used *Sentence Construction* and *Sentence Combination* and offered constructive ideas for using and improving them. These helpful colleagues are simply too numerous to name, but we thank them all.

Fortunate is the teacher who works at a school where the administration encourages creativity in teaching and promotes the development of new materials that better fit students' educational needs. For support of this nature, we are grateful to the administration of Brigham Young University–Hawaii. In particular, we thank the directors of its English Language Institute, Earl Wyman and Norman Evans, who allowed the trial use of preliminary revisions of *Sentence Construction* and *Sentence Combination* in ELI courses for several semesters.

Special appreciation is due to various members of the Newbury House and the Heinle & Heinle editorial staffs who helped us through the long process of producing this second edition: Laurie Likoff, who got us started; Kathleen Ossip, who kept us going; and David Lee and Anne Sokolsky, who saw things through to completion.

The comments of the reviewers of the semifinal revised manuscript were also very helpful and much appreciated. Therefore, we wish to thank: Ulysses D'Aguila (Alemany Community College), Christine Bauer-Ramazani (St. Michael's College), Ellen Lewin (Minneapolis Community College), Ann Ludwig (University of Nebraska), Monica Maxwell (Georgetown University), and Mark Picus (Houston Community College).

Finally, we extend our deepest thanks to our families for their endless patience and cheerful sacrifices. This section would be deplorably incomplete if it failed to acknowledge the unflagging support and willing assistance of Terumi, Cristina, Daniel, Linda, and James during the years it took to complete the revision.

L.E.H.
A.C.P.

8
Modifiers

This chapter will help you avoid or correct mistakes like these:

- For Christmas he got a <u>red new</u> bicycle.
- This school is <u>too</u> big that if you meet somebody you may never see that person again.
- Air pollution is now <u>lowest</u> than before.
- Her <u>closer</u> neighbor lives about one kilometer away.
- She is very <u>interesting</u> in everything related to English.
- She likes <u>a lot</u> to hear music.
- She went back to study <u>to California</u>.
- Here my English was weak compared to <u>the other high school</u>.
- Learning English in my country is different <u>from BYU</u>.

1. The Nucleus of the Noun Phrase

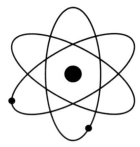

Every subject or object noun phrase has one main noun. In this book it is called the *nucleus*. Verbs, aux-words, and pronouns agree with this nucleus (or main noun). Other words may be used to modify the nucleus. The resulting group of words is not a sentence, but a noun phrase. Words used to modify nouns are usually called adjectives. Words used to modify verbs and other modifiers are usually called adverbs. The forms of adjectives and adverbs are explained in Chapter 1 (in Book I, *Sentence Construction*).

2. Order of Noun Modifiers

2.1   Single-word modifiers precede the nucleus.

> The **globe**.
> The world **globe**.
> The large world **globe**.
> The large multi-colored world **globe**.

2.2   When more than one single-word modifier is used, they follow a set order. See the chart on page 3 for this order. This order is changed only when special emphasis is given to one modifier. In writing, an emphasized out-of-place modifier is often underlined (italicized).

2.3   When the nucleus is a **singular count noun** or **group noun**, one (and only one) of the following modifiers **must** be used: an article (explained in Chapter 2), a demonstrative, a possessive, or the word *one*.
    The articles *a/an* and the determiners *each* and *every* are used to modify **singular count** nouns only. The demonstratives *this* and *that* may be used with **noncount** nouns also.
    With **noncount** or **plural count nouns**, articles, demonstratives, or possessives may or may not be used.

2.4   All single word modifiers do **not always** modify the nucleus. They may modify other modifiers.

> The South American businessman

In this noun phrase, *South* modifies *American*, while the combination *South American* modifies the nucleus *businessman*.

2.5   When two or more single-word, nucleus modifiers (in columns III to VII on the chart on page 3) occur together, they are usually separated by commas. A simple test to determine if a comma is needed is to place the word *and* between the two adjectives. If *and* can be used, then the comma is correct.

Order of Noun Modifiers

		SINGLE-WORD MODIFIERS							NOUN	PHRASES AND CLAUSES	
I	II	III	IV	V	VI	VII	VIII	NUCLEUS	IX	X
Pre-article	1. Articles and Indefinite Adjectives 2. Demonstratives 3. Possessives	Numerals 1. Ordinal 2. Cardinal	Superlative and Comparative Markers	1. General Size 2. Quality or Characteristic 3. General Weight	1. Specific Size 2. Shape 3. Age 4. Temperature 5. Specific Weight	1. Time 2. Color 3. Location 4. Origin or Nationality	Nouns used as Adjectives	NUCLEUS	Modifying Phrases	Modifying Clauses (See Chapter 12, section 2)
Both Only	the			tired	old	Indian		men	sitting there	
	the		least	difficult			algebra	problem		that we did
	The	first two						chapters	in the book	
	These	four		little		brown		rocks		
	Her	first			new		application	job		
	John's			surprising			plastic	attitude		that you saw
	The man's		less	impressive			picture	form		
	My brother's		more	big	six foot	blue		chair		
	Many			expensive	rectangular	black		frames	from New York	
	A				cold	Alaskan	winter	day		
		Six		rich		American		tourists	carrying cameras	who talk loudly
	Those					weekly	news	magazines		which came today
All	the	twenty	most	beautiful	new	red	water	beds	with leaks	that I fixed

Note: Only one modifier from column II can be used at a time.

If the nucleus is singular, then a modifier from column II must be used.

If the nucleus is plural, then a modifier from column II may or may not be used.

> The four little (and) brown rocks
> The four little, brown rocks
>
> The least difficult algebra problem
> (because *least* modifies *difficult*, no comma is used)

EXERCISE 2-A   *Rearrange the modifiers (in parentheses) into their proper order.*

A DANGEROUS VOYAGE

[1]Last year, (cold, water-soaked, five, tired) men battled (storm-tossed, Atlantic, the, dangerous) Ocean in (leather, a, fragile, small) vessel to prove that (Atlantic, northern, ancient, an) voyage could have been made. [2](adventurous, brave, the) crew of (leather, small, the) craft successfully sailed across (perilous, the, icy, northern, Atlantic) Ocean despite (the, ice, large) floes and (rocky, hazardous, the) shorelines. [3](heroic, this, superhuman) feat once again shows us that humans can battle (hostile, unknown, a/an) environment and win.

EXERCISE 2-B   *Rearrange the modifiers (in parentheses) into their proper order.*

STRANGE SIGHTS

[1]Not long ago, on (stormy, a, dark) night, I saw (strange, many, frightening) sights. [2]I could hardly believe my eyes. [3]It started when my doorbell rang. [4]When I opened the door, there was (a, green, large, hideous) dinosaur with (grinning, a, wide) mouth and (tapering, a, long, scaly) tail smiling at me. [5]I quickly slammed the door and locked it. [6]Then I ran to the window and looked out. [7]To my horror, I saw (gray, furry, four) werewolves running down the sidewalk. [8]In the neighbor's yard, there was (a, grinning, silent, pale) vampire with (white, long, two, pointed) fangs protruding from his mouth. [9]While I watched, (muscular, a, six-foot, hairy) gorilla came walking across the street. [10]Not far behind, there was (a, beautiful, little) ballerina wearing (pink, shining, a) dress and holding (long, a, magic) wand in her hand. [11]My doorbell rang again, and when I peeked out, I saw (short, a, cackling, ugly) witch with (tall, a, black, pointed) hat and (red, long, curved) fingernails, which looked like claws. [12]For a while, I thought I had gone completely crazy. [13]Or perhaps I was having a nightmare. [14]Then I remembered. [15]It was Halloween, the holiday when children put on masks and costumes and go from door to door saying, "Trick or treat."

EXERCISE 2-C   *Rearrange the modifiers (in parentheses) into their proper order.*

RECORDS

[1]For (strange, any, fantastic) facts about records, consult (gigantic, amazing, new, the) edition of the *Guinness Book of Records*. [2]It is (reliable, best-known, the, international, reference) book available for (authentic, the, record-breaking) achievements of men and women. [3]It lists (natural, fantastic, many) phenomena, such as (known, the, greatest, volcanic) explosion, (most, active, southerly, the) volcano, (lava, longest, the) flow, and (prehistoric, the, known, lava, largest) flow. [4]In addition, (racing, fastest, world's, the) car, (production, fastest, the) cars, and (powerful, most, piston-engined, world's, the) car are also named.

3. Singular and Plural Forms of Modifiers

Only the demonstratives have singular and plural forms. All other modifiers have only one form—*singular*—although they may be used with singular or plural nouns.

This ruler is two *feet* long.	It is a two-*foot* ruler.
The boy is three *years* old.	He is a three-*year*-old boy.
The building is forty *stories* high.	It is a forty-*story* building.

Note: A hyphen is normally used between each of the words in a group of words which acts as a single modifier.

4. Adjective Complement Modifiers

When an adjective complement (sentence pattern number three or four) forms part of one or more related sentences with a nucleus noun in common, the sentences may be *combined* by using the adjective complements as single-word modifiers.

Simple	Combined
The room was dark. The room scared Sheila.	The dark room scared Sheila.
The trees were green. The trees were beautiful. They cut down the trees.	They cut down the beautiful green trees.

EXERCISE 4-A

Change the sentences under each main sentence into single-word adjectives. Place these adjectives in the main sentence before the nouns they modify. Then write the modified sentences in paragraph form.

ATHLETICS

1. Fans admire an athlete.
    The fans are sports-minded.
    The athlete is successful.

2. However, people realize the effort required to succeed in the field of athletics.
    The people are few.
    The effort is tremendous.
    The field is competitive.

3. Athletes must forgo pleasures.
    The athletes are great.
    The pleasures are many.

4. They must develop self-discipline.
    The self-discipline is great.

5. A training period is not unusual.
  The training period is intensive.
  The training period is six months.

6. They spend hours in exercise.
  The hours are countless.
  The exercise is grueling.

7. They must eat food.
  The food is nutritious.

8. Cooperation with coaches is vital for success.
  The cooperation is constant.
  The coaches are different.
  The success is athletic.

9. An athlete must develop a spirit.
  The athlete is dedicated.
  The spirit is competitive.

10. Success in sports is achieved only through effort.
  The sports are competitive.
  The effort is constant.
  The effort is consistent.

EXERCISE 4-B   *Change the sentences under each main sentence into single-word adjectives. Place these adjectives in the main sentence before the nouns they modify. Then write the modified sentences in paragraph form.*

AN ESSAY

1. To write an essay, one must begin with sentences.
  The essay is acceptable.
  The essay is two pages.
  The sentences are basic.

2. Sentences require words in syntax.
  The sentences are good.
  The sentences are basic.
  The syntax is correct.

3. Sentences are then combined into paragraphs.
  The sentences are related.
  The paragraphs are topical.

4. Essays depend on sentences.
  The essays are well written.
  The sentences are error-free.

5. Students recognize this.
  The students are good.

6. Students learn to write sentences.
  The students are conscientious.
  The sentences are correct.
  The sentences are grammatical.

7. Then they learn ways to combine their sentences.
  The ways are different.
  The sentences are supporting.

8. They center each paragraph around a sentence.
   The paragraphs are individual.
   The sentences are topical.

9. All material is eliminated.
   The material is extraneous.

10. Paragraphs make essays.
    The paragraphs are informative.
    The essays are interesting.

EXERCISE 4-C   *Change the sentences under each main sentence into single-word adjectives. Place these adjectives in the main sentence before the nouns they modify. Then write the modified sentences in paragraph form.*

A GARDEN

1. The gardener receives rewards.
   The gardener is an amateur.
   The rewards are many.

2. A garden makes a yard.
   The garden is lovely.
   The yard is nice-looking.

3. Vegetables for meals are a bonus.
   The vegetables are fresh.
   The meals are healthful.
   The bonus is great.

4. A bouquet of flowers for a house is another bonus.
   The bouquet is lovely.
   The house is well kept.
   The bonus is fine.

5. These benefits do not come without effort.
   The benefits are good.
   The effort is great.

6. The gardener makes sacrifices.
   The gardener is successful.
   The sacrifices are many.

7. Effort is necessary to raise a garden.
   The effort is persistent.
   The garden is good.

8. Watering and weeding are chores.
   The watering and weeding are constant.
   The chores are necessary.

9. There is warfare against bugs.
   The warfare is continual.
   The bugs are plant-destroying.
   The bugs are voracious.

10. The gardener feels that the satisfaction more than compensates for the effort
    to raise a garden.
    The gardener is successful.
    The satisfaction is personal.
    The garden is successful.
    The effort lasts four months.

5. Verb Forms Used as Modifiers

5.1 The timeless *d-t-n* and *-ing* forms of many (but not all) verbs are often used as **adjectives**. In these cases, they are **not verbs** and are not preceded by aux-words. In other words, the rules for aux-words and verb forms explained in Chapters 4 and 5 do not apply when these verb forms are used as modifiers.

5.2 To know which form (*d-t-n* or *-ing*) of the verb to use as a modifier, create a "basic sentence" (pattern one or pattern two [see Chapter 7]) which uses the modifying verb form as its main verb. In this basic sentence, the noun which the verb form modifies in the noun phrase will become either the subject (the *doer* of the action) or object (the *receiver* of the action), depending on the meaning.

> I am $\left\langle \begin{array}{c} \text{exciting (?)} \\ \text{excited (?)} \end{array} \right\rangle$ about the party.
>
> Basic sentence: The party excites me.

5.3 If the noun is the **subject** of the basic sentence (i.e., the *doer* of the action), then use the *-ing* form of the verb to modify it.

> **The party** excites me. = The party is exci**ting**.
> (subject)

Basic Sentence	Noun Phrase with Modifier
The class bores the students.	The boring class
The boy runs.	The running boy
The fireworks explode.	The exploding fireworks
The news amazed the people.	The amazing news
The band thrilled the audience.	The thrilling band

5.4 If the noun is the **object** of the basic sentence (i.e., the *receiver* of the action), then use the *d-t-n* form of the verb to modify it.

> The party excites **me**. = I am excit**ed**.

Basic Sentence	Noun Phrase with Modifier
The class bores the students.	The bored students
The news amazed the people.	The amazed people
The band thrilled the audience.	The thrilled audience

5.5 The noun phrases with *-ing* or *d-t-n* modifiers formed in this way can be used in any noun position in another sentence.

The boring class had only a few students.
    (subject)

Few students attended *the boring class*.
                         (object)

Dietetics 679 was *a boring class*.
             (complement)

Only a few students made it through *the boring class*.
                              (object of preposition)

The bored students suffered through the class.
  (subject)

The professor ignored *the bored students*.
                     (object)

I was *a bored student*.
  (complement)

EXERCISE 5-A   *Change each of the "basic sentences" below into a noun phrase with a modifier by writing the correct form of the modifier in the blank. (Note: Some of the modifiers are not* d-t-n *or* -ing *forms of verbs but simple adjective complements, as explained in section 4 of this chapter.)*

EMPLOYERS AND EMPLOYEES

1. The work interests the men.

The _____ work

The _____ men

2. The work is hard.

The _____ work

3. The work tires the employees.

The _____ work

The _____ employees

4. The supervisors are helpful.

The _____ supervisors

5. The employees work hard.

The _____ employees

6. The employers pay the workers well.

The _____ workers

The _____ employers

7. The workers are busy.

The _____ workers

8. The employees deserve praise.

The _____ employees

9. The managers praise the employees.

The _____ employees

The _____ managers

10. The employer-employee team is harmonious.

The _____ employer-employee team

EXERCISE 5-B   *Change each of the "basic sentences" below into a noun phrase with a modifier by writing the correct form of the modifier in the blank. (Note: Some of the modifiers are not* d-t-n *or* -ing *forms of verbs but simple adjective complements, as explained in section 4 of this chapter.)*

THE THEATER

1. The performance thrills the audience.

The _____ audience

The _____ performance

2. The dancers dazzle the viewers.

The _____ dancers

The _____ viewers

3. The costumes disgust the critics.

The _____ costumes

The _____ critics

4. The program confuses the readers.

The _____ readers

The _____ program

5. The music soothes the listeners.

The _____ music

The _____ listeners

6. The atmosphere is pleasant.

The _____ atmosphere

7. The lights illuminate the stage.

The _____ lights

The _____ stage

8. The actors perform.

The _____ actors

9. The play interests the audience.

The _____ play

The _____ audience

10. The show pleases the people.

The _____ people

The _____ show

EXERCISE 5-C   *Change each of the "basic sentences" below into a noun phrase with a modifier by writing the correct form of the modifier in the blank.*

ELECTIONS

1. Elections come soon.

The _____ elections

2. The voters choose a president.

The _____ president

The _____ voters

3. Many candidates vie for office.

The _____ candidates

The _____ office

4. The candidates harangue the populace.

The _____ populace

The _____ candidates

5. The people suffer the speeches silently.

The _____ people

The _____ speeches

6. The voters declare their choice.

The _____ choice

The _____ voters

7. One candidate wins.

The _____ candidate

8. Other candidates lose the election.

The _____ candidates

The _____ election

9. The voters select another president.

The _____ president

The _____ voters

10. The people rule.

The _____ people

6. Comparative Forms of Adjectives

6.1   Adjectives and adverbs are used to describe qualities. When two things share a **common quality**, it is possible to compare them. Comparative forms of adjectives are used to make such comparisons.

(trees that share a common characteristic: tallness)

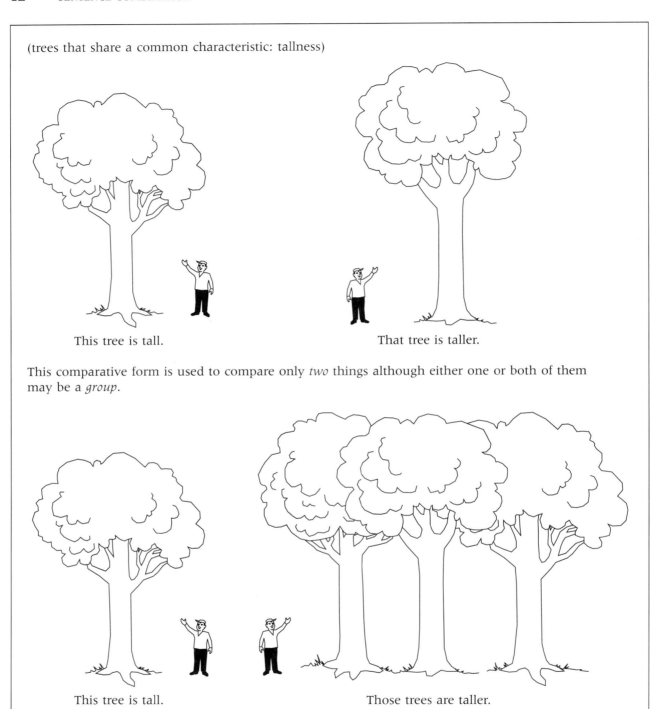

This tree is tall.

That tree is taller.

This comparative form is used to compare only *two* things although either one or both of them may be a *group*.

This tree is tall.

Those trees are taller.

6.2 Comparative forms are made by adding the suffix *-er* to one-syllable adjectives.

Last week's test was hard. This week's test was *harder*.
Bill is fat. John is *fatter*. (notice the double consonant)

The word *more* is placed before adjectives of *three or more* syllables.

> Last week's test was difficult. This week's test was *more* difficult.

Many (but *not all*) two-syllable adjectives may add *-er* or use the word *more* to make the comparative form.

> Last week's test was tricky.
> This week's test was *trickier*. OR
> This week's test was *more tricky*.

Note: *Only one* of these two methods (*more* or *-er*) may be used at a time.

> **Wrong** → This week's test was *more trickier*.

d-t-n forms and *-ing* verb forms used as modifiers (discussed in section 5 of this chapter) always use *more* for comparison.

> That class was interesting.
> This class is *more interesting*.
> David is bored, but his brother is *more bored*.

There are a few irregular comparative forms.

> The comparative form for *good* is *better*.
> The comparative form for *well* is *better* also.
> The comparative form for *bad* is *worse*.
> The comparative form for *little* is *less*.
> The comparative form for *much* (noncount nouns) is *more*.
> The comparative form for *many* (count nouns) is *more* also.

6.3 Two sentences can be combined into one comparative sentence by using the word *than*. The predicate in the second sentence is usually deleted. However, the aux-word may be retained.

> This tree is tall. That tree is taller. → That tree is taller than this tree (is tall).
> I am tall. He is taller. → He is taller than I am (tall).

When such comparative sentences are constructed, the comparison must involve two things of the same type which share a common quality.

> **Wrong** → Learning Chinese in China is easier than the United States.
> (comparing learning Chinese with the United States)
> **Right** → Learning Chinese is harder than learning English.
> (comparing learning Chinese with learning English)

EXERCISE 6-A   *Answer the following questions with an answer that gives a comparison. Use a different comparison for each answer. Be sure that your answer makes sense and that you compare the same sorts of things.*

WRITING ENGLISH

Models:
   Was the lesson long?   It was longer than the last one.
   Was the subject interesting?   It was more interesting than most subjects.

1. Is English difficult?

2. Is writing English easy?

3. Are the grammar rules complex?

4. Is the word order complicated?

5. Are the vocabulary words hard?

6. Is your pronunciation bad?

7. Do you practice often?

8. Is your text good?

9. Is your teacher prepared?

EXERCISE 6-B   *Answer the following questions with an answer that gives a comparison. Use a different comparison for each answer. Be sure that your answer makes sense and that you compare the same sorts of things.*

FOOTBALL FEVER

1. Was the football game tough?

2. Did the players seem rough?

   3. Was the field wet?

   4. Did the coach keep calm?

   5. Were the winners happy?

   6. Were the losers angry?

   7. Were the referees fair?

   8. Was the stadium full?

   9. Were the spectators interested?

 10. Were the cheerleaders peppy?

EXERCISE 6-C *Answer the following questions with an answer that gives a comparison. Use a different comparison for each answer. Be sure that your answer makes sense and that you compare the same sorts of things.*

AN UNFAMILIAR COUNTRY

   1. Is the country green?

   2. Is the country hot?

   3. Are the towns small?

   4. Are the people happy?

   5. Are the roads bad?

   6. Is the scenery beautiful?

   7. Is the water warm?

   8. Are the mountains rugged?

9. Is the harbor deep?

10. Is food plentiful?

7. Superlative Forms of Adjectives

7.1   Superlative forms of adjectives are used to compare one thing with all other things in its "reference group." The superlative is used to describe the one member of a group which exceeds all other things in that group in a specific, shared quality.

This is *the tallest* tree in the forest.

The article *the* normally precedes the superlative forms of adjectives.

Susan is **the** *smartest* girl in *the class*.

7.2   The reference group is not always stated in the sentence, but it must be clear either from the context or a previous reference.

There are many smart girls in our class. Susan is the smartest.
   (previous reference = "our class")
This is the hardest test we've had all semester.
   (context = "of all the tests during the semester")

7.3   The superlative form is made by adding the suffix *-est* to a one-syllable adjective. The word *most* is placed before an adjective of three or more syllables. Many (but *not all*) two-syllable adjectives may add *-est* or use the word *most* to make the superlative form.

> The tallest building in the world is the Sears Tower in Chicago. This is the most interesting book I have ever read.

EXERCISE 7-A

Study the data below. Then write ten sentences using comparatives and five sentences using superlatives based on the data.

The Continents of the World—Areas and Populations over the Years

CONTINENT	AREA		POPULATION			
	Square Miles	% of Earth	1650	1850	1990	% of 1990 Total
Africa	11,700,000	20.2%	100,000,000	95,000,000	795,000,000	14.9%
Antarctica	5,400,000	9.3%	uninhabited	uninhabited	uninhabited	0%
Asia	17,300,000	30.1%	335,000,000	754,000,000	3,135,000,000	58.7%
Europe	3,800,000	6.6%	100,000,000	265,000,000	649,000,000	12.1%
North America	9,400,000	16.2%	5,000,000	39,000,000	277,000,000	5.1%
Oceania*	3,300,000	5.7%	2,000,000	2,000,000	26,000,000	0.4%
South America	6,900,000	11.9%	8,000,000	20,000,000	450,000,000	8.4%

*Includes Australia

EXERCISE 7-B

Study the data below. Then write ten sentences using comparatives and five sentences using superlatives based on the data.

Information on the Planets

	Mercury	Venus	Earth	Mars	Jupiter	Saturn	Uranus	Neptune	Pluto
Average Distance from the sun (million miles)	36.0	67.2	92.9	141.5	483.4	886.0	1,782	2,792	3,664
Equatorial Diameter (miles)	3,100	7,700	7,927	4,220	88,100	75,100	29,200	27,700	8,700
Mean Orbital Velocity (miles per second)	29.76	21.78	18.52	14.49	8.1	6.0	4.2	3.4	3.0
Mean Surface Gravity	.36	.87	1.00	.38	2.64	1.13	1.07	1.41	—

EXERCISE 7-C

Study the following data. Then write ten sentences using comparatives and five sentences using superlatives based on the data. (Remember that the article the is not usually used with the names of lakes when they are singular, but it is used with the names of seas. The use of articles with proper nouns is explained in Chapter 2, section 7, and Chapter 8, section 2.3 and section 7.1.)

Ten Major Lakes of the World

Name	Continent	Area (in square miles)	Length (in miles)	Depth (in feet)	Elevation (in feet above or below sea level)
Caspian Sea*	Asia-Europe	143,244	760	3,363	−92
Lake Superior	North America	31,700	350	1,330	600
Lake Victoria	Africa	26,828	250	270	3,720
Aral Sea*	Asia	24,904	280	220	174
Lake Huron	North America	23,000	206	750	579
Lake Michigan	North America	22,300	307	923	579
Lake Tanganyika	Africa	12,700	420	4,823	2,534
Lake Baykal	Asia	12,162	395	5,315	1,493
Great Bear Lake	North America	12,096	192	1,463	512
Lake Malawi	Africa	11,150	360	2,280	1,550

*By definition, a lake is a body of standing water completely surrounded by land. Despite their names, the Caspian Sea and the Aral Sea fit this definition, so they are included in this list.

8. Nouns Used as Adjectives

8.1   Nouns can be used as adjectives. (In this case, they are sometimes called noun adjuncts). In these cases it is important not to confuse them with the nucleus of the noun phrase. The verb following the noun phrase must agree with the *nucleus*, and *not* with the noun used as an adjective!

8.2   Nouns used as adjectives are usually placed directly *before* the nucleus.

The old *metal* tables are getting rusty.

(The word *tables* is the nucleus. The word *metal* modifies *tables* by telling what they are made of.)

Snow tires are useful during *winter* weather.

(*snow* modifies *tires*)(*winter* modifies *weather*)

This *algebra* problem seems hard.

(*algebra* modifies *problem*)

---

9. Phrases and Clauses Used as Adjectives

9.1   Modifiers that consist of more than one word (phrases and clauses) are placed *after* the noun they modify (the nucleus of the noun phrase).

9.2   Modifying phrases may be prepositional phrases or half-sentences. (Half-sentences are discussed in Chapter 11.) These modifying phrases contain nouns. The nouns may have their own sets of modifiers. The nouns in these modifying phrases should *not* be confused with the nucleus of the entire noun phrase!

The curtains *in the front room* are blue and orange.

(The aux-word *are* agrees with the plural nucleus *curtains, not* with the singular *room* in the modifying phrase.)

The students *sitting in the front row* always work hard.

(The no *-s* form *work* is used because the nucleus *students* is plural.)

9.3 Modifying clauses (discussed in Chapter 12, section 2) also follow the nucleus noun (and any modifying phrases). They contain nouns and verbs which must *not* be confused with the nucleus of the noun phrase and the verb of the predicate.

The chorus *that came from State College* yesterday gave a great performance.

The lion *that escaped from the zoo* was running along the sidewalk.

EXERCISE 9-A   *In the passage below, the longer noun phrases have been marked like this: -(noun phrase)-   Circle the nucleus of each noun phrase. Underline each of the words, phrases, or clauses that modify the nucleus. Then draw arrows from each of the modifiers to the nucleus. The first one has been done for you as an example.*

WATER

¹-(A large (part) of the human body)- is water. ²Water helps to protect -(the body cells)- by acting as -(a cushion.)- ³-(The body)- maintains -(a fairly constant water content)- by balancing -(the water intake)- with -(water loss.)- ⁴It loses -(some water)- when we perspire, and that helps to regulate -(body temperature.)- ⁵Thirst is -(one of the signals that the body needs water.)- ⁶While humans can survive -(the lack of food and other nutrients)- for weeks or sometimes even months, we can live for -(only a few days)- without water. ⁷It is -(a necessary part of all body fluids such as blood, digestive juices, and body wastes.)-

⁸All foods contain water. ⁹By drinking liquids and eating -(a wide variety of foods)- throughout the day, -(the human body)- can carry on -(normal functions.)-

EXERCISE 9-B   *In the passage below, the longer noun phrases have been marked like this: -(noun phrase)-   Circle the nucleus of each noun phrase. Underline each of the words, phrases, or clauses that modify the nucleus. Then draw arrows from each of the modifiers to the nucleus.*

POLICE WORK*

¹-(Police work)- is often exceedingly difficult. ²-(The combination of pressures on the present-day urban police department)- is tremendous. ³Frustrations stem from -(poor pay,)- -(inadequate training,)- -(limited opportunity,)- -(long

hours,)- -(public antipathy,)- and -(difficult, sometimes dangerous work.)- [4]-(Intense pressures from business and civic groups frightened by crime)- are -(the lot of a policeman.)- [5]Frustration is caused by the press, -(civil liberty groups,)- the courts, and the bureaucracy. [6]A policeman must contend with -(public demand for greater use of force,)- -(isolation from suburban people,)- -(college students,)- and -(minority groups.)- [7]-(All of the emotionalism of the public concern over crime)- focuses on the police.

*Adapted from Ramsey Clark, *Crime in America* (New York: Simon and Schuster, 1970).

EXERCISE 9-C   *In the passage below, the longer noun phrases have been marked like this: -(noun phrase)-   Circle the nucleus of each noun phrase. Underline each of the words, phrases, or clauses that modify the nucleus. Then draw arrows from each of the modifiers to the nucleus.*

BAD DEAL AT THE TRADING POST*

[1]-(More than 50% of America's farm products)- today consists of -(plants used by the Indians before Columbus planted his flag.)- [2]They include beans, chocolate, corn, cotton, peanuts, potatoes, pumpkins, tobacco, and tomatoes. [3]Botanists have yet to discover, in 400 years, -(any medicinal herb that was not used by the Indian.)- [4]That's what they gave us.

[5]Here's -(what we have given them:)- -(high infant mortality rate,)- -(short life expectancy,)- -(dependency on handouts,)- -(loss of pride,)- -(much illness,)- and -(unemployment as high as 80% in some tribes.)- [6]-(The remaining American Indians)- are struggling to hang on to -(the lowest health, education, and economic rungs in American life.)- [7]Somebody had better do something before -(those rungs)- collapse. [8]Remember you're up there somewhere on -(that ladder)- yourself.

*"Bad Deal at the Trading Post," *Newsweek*, February 17, 1969, p. 91. Used by permission.

10. Adverbs of Frequency and Probability

10.1   Adverbs are words that modify verbs, adjectives, and other adverbs. Adverbs may be added to any basic sentence pattern. The proper place to put them depends on the type of adverb.

10.2   **Adverbs of frequency** modify the verb of the sentence. These adverbs show different degrees of frequency. (Adverbs of frequency answer the question "How often?") Here are some common adverbs of frequency:

always	occasionally
usually	seldom
often	rarely
frequently	never
sometimes	

Adverbs of frequency are placed in front of time-included verb forms but imme-diately after time-included aux-words.

> Reuben *usually* goes at eight o'clock.
> He *never* misses class.
> He is *seldom* late.
> He has *always* been prompt.

10.3   **Adverbs of probability** may also be used in this position. Here are some common adverbs of probability:

apparently	obviously
certainly	possibly
clearly	probably
evidently	surely

> He will *certainly* come. (great probability)
> He will *probably* come. (some probability)

They may also be used before the aux-word and, if emphasis is desired, as front shifters.

> He certainly will come.
> Certainly, he will come.

EXERCISE 10-A   *Write ten sentences about* **your daily routine.** *Include at least one adverb of frequency or probability in each sentence. Underline the adverbs.*

EXERCISE 10-B   *Write ten sentences about* **your normal weekend activities.** *Include at least one adverb of frequency or probability in each sentence. Underline the adverbs.*

EXERCISE 10-C   *Write ten sentences about* **what your teacher does in class.** *Include at least one adverb of frequency or probability in each sentence. Underline the adverbs.*

11. Adverbs of Intensity

11.1   **Adverbs of intensity** modify adjectives or other adverbs. They are used to make the meaning of these adjectives or adverbs stronger or more forceful.
Two very common adverbs of intensity are *very* and *extremely*. They are placed immediately before the adjective or adverb they modify.

> I am *extremely* tired.
> The package is *very* big.

11.2 *Too* is an intensifier with a special use. It suggests an undesirable excess of the adjective. It is frequently followed by a phrase beginning with the word *to* (sometimes *for*).

> I am *too* tired *to* play football.

11.3 *So* is another special intensifier. In writing it is usually followed by a clause beginning with the word *that*.

> They were *so* happy *that* they cried.

11.4 Although *so* and *too* are both intensifiers and seem to have similar meanings, the phrases/clauses that follow them have **opposite** meanings. Notice in the examples below that the *that* clauses have negative aux-words to make them have the same meaning as the *to* phrases.

> I'm *too* tired *to* work anymore.
> I'm *so* tired *that* I *can't* work anymore.
>
> The package is *too* big *to* fit in the mailbox.
> The package is *so* big *that* it *won't* fit in the mailbox.

EXERCISE 11-A *Write two additional sentences, one using* too *and one using* so *for each sentence below. Follow the pattern given in the model. Write sentences that fit the topic.*

DOMESTIC DIFFICULTIES

Model:
  Last night Father was very tired.
  Last night Father was *too* tired to eat supper.
  Last night Father was *so* tired that he couldn't eat.

1. Mother was very busy.

2. The children were very noisy.

3. Mother and Father became very upset.

4. Father shouted very loudly.

5. Mother scolded the children very quietly.

6. Suddenly the house was very quiet.

EXERCISE 11-B

Write two additional sentences, one using too *and one using* so, *for each sentence below. Follow the pattern given in the model. Write sentences that fit the topic.*

A GOOD MOVIE

Model:
   Last week I saw a very good movie.
   The movie was *too* good to miss.
   The movie was *so* good that I want to see it again.

   1. The film was very short.

   2. The plot was very scary.

   3. The photography was very unusual.

   4. The actors were very talented.

   5. The theater was very full.

   6. The show was very good.

   7. The audience clapped very loudly.

EXERCISE 11-C

Write two additional sentences, one using too *and one using* so, *for each sentence below. Follow the pattern given in the model. Write sentences that fit the topic.*

AN EXCITING FOOTBALL GAME

Model:
   A football game is very exciting.
   A football game is *too* exciting for some people to watch.
   A football game is *so* exciting that I scream and yell.

   1. The players are very strong.

   2. The quarterback passes the ball very swiftly.

   3. The linesmen tackle the opposing players very hard.

   4. Sometimes the football is very slippery.

   5. The football field is very large.

   6. When their team wins, the spectators are very happy.

12. Adverbs of Manner, Place, Time, etc.

12.1   **Adverbs of manner** are used to modify verbs and adjectives made from -*ing* or *d-t-n* forms of verbs (see section 5 of this chapter). These adverbs are normally placed after the verb, or after the object if there is an object. (The alternate position, for emphasizing the adverb, is before the verb. For example, "She learned quickly," becomes "She quickly learned," when the speed is emphasized.)

Most adverbs of manner are formed by adding -*ly* to an adjective. (A few adverbs of manner such as *fast* and *hard* do not end in -*ly*, and *well* is the adverb form of *good*.)

Here are some common adverbs of manner:

quickly	suddenly
slowly	thoroughly
carefully	stealthily
wildly	smoothly
precisely	boldly

> To write English *well* you must write *carefully*.
> She gave the speech *quickly*.
> The cat crept *stealthily* toward the bird.
> The *smoothly* running water flowed over the dam.

12.2   Adverbs of manner (and a few adverbs of frequency) also have **comparative** and **superlative** forms. Adverbs ending in -*ly* always use *more* and *most* for forming comparatives and superlatives. Single-word adverbs add -*er* and -*est*. The rules for using these forms are the same as those for using comparative and superlative adjective forms. (These are discussed in sections 6 and 7 of this chapter.)

> George runs fast, but Mary runs *faster*.
> Mr. Jones reacts quickly, but Mr. Jackson reacts *more quickly*.
> I frequently go to town, but George goes *more frequently*.

12.3   **Adverbs of place and time** are usually prepositional phrases. (Some exceptions are *here, there, home, everywhere, anywhere,* and *somewhere* for place, and *yesterday, now,* and *then* for time.)

Here are some common adverbial time expressions:

in the morning	after lunch
at night	before breakfast
in the winter	during the semester
since 1933	next week

Like adverbs of manner, adverbs of place and time are normally placed after the verb or object.

> I went shopping *at ten o'clock.*
> I saw Mary *in the supermarket.*

12.4   When more than one kind (manner, place, or time) of adverb is used, the normal order is **manner** followed by **place** followed by **time**.

> I saw Mary *in the supermarket* (**place**) *at ten o'clock* (**time**).
> George studies *frantically* (**manner**) *in the library* (**place**) *during the last week of the semester* (**time**).

12.5   Other prepositional phrases which show **means, instrument,** and **purpose** are used as adverbs also. They normally go at the end of the sentence.

means	He travels *by train.*
instrument	He made his purchase *with a credit card.*
purpose	He crams *for the test.*

EXERCISE 12-A   *Insert adverbs of the type indicated in the proper (normal) place in each sentence.*

SPORTS ON TV

1. People have some kind of recreation. (frequency)
2. A few people participate in active sports. (frequency)
3. The majority prefer to sit and watch others play. (place)
4. Thousands travel to watch football games. (frequency and place)
5. Thousands more watch the same games on TV. (manner and place)
6. Admittance to the stadium requires a ticket. (frequency)
7. Sponsors pay for TV broadcasting. (frequency)
8. Companies advertise their products during time-outs. (manner)
9. The only cost for watching is the price of the TV set. (place)
10. Of course, TV watchers have to endure the commercials. (manner or place)

EXERCISE 12-B   *Insert adverbs of the types indicated in the proper (normal) place in each sentence.*

THE OLYMPIC GAMES

1. The Olympic Games take place. (frequency and place)
2. Specific cities or countries provide the facilities. (manner)
3. Summer and winter games attract many people. (manner)
4. Amateur athletes from all over the world perform. (manner)
5. These athletes prepare. (manner and time)
6. They train hard. (intensity)

7. Spectators watch the various events. (manner)

8. Athletes break world records. (frequency and place)

9. The decathlon champion is the world's finest all-around athlete. (probability)

10. Money for the athletes' expenses comes from private donations. (frequency)

EXERCISE 12-C   *Rewrite the following sentences inserting adverbs of the types indicated in the proper (normal) place in each sentence.*

MY SECRET TALENT

1. I sleep with my eyes closed. (frequency, manner, place, and time)

2. I am also able to sleep with my eyes open. (frequency, and time or place)

3. Few people can do this. (manner)

4. It is my greatest talent. (probability)

5. This talent is useful to me. (intensity)

6. I couldn't live without it. (probability)

7. When things are interesting, I listen and watch. (manner)

8. When boredom sets in, I go to sleep. (frequency and manner)

9. Because I don't close my eyes, those around me don't suspect that I am asleep. (frequency)

10. My only problem is that I snore. (frequency)

11. If I start to snore, those around me discover my secret. (frequency and manner)

9

Compounding

This chapter will help you combine simple sentences and their parts correctly while avoiding or correcting mistakes like these:

- He must be punished or give him a warning.
- Dr. McAllen was chosen to head the delegation to China because of his experience traveling in the Far East and had also lived there for two years and also knows many important people there.
- Snakes have killed many people in the forests and in the jungles even in the deserts.
- Some people think snakes are very attractive, I strongly disagree.
- During *fiesta* you can see everybody in action, most of them want to work.
- They think I am not of Hawaiian descent but certainly I would have brown skin.
- If you study hard, you will achieve good grades and successful.
- He studies a lot, and so is his roommate.
- My friends couldn't find the book, and neither the librarian could.
- Our class visited the state capital, the art museum, and ate sack lunches in the park.

1. Compounding Sentence Parts

1.1   Simple, basic sentences that are related may be combined into complex sentences in a number of ways. The most common way to combine two or more related, basic sentences (or their parts) is by compounding them.

Compounding sentence parts is a little bit like connecting up cars in a train.

1.2   When two or more sentences have **different subjects** but the **same predicate**, the subjects may be compounded by using the words *and* or *or*. This compounding process results in one sentence.

   When *and* is used, the resulting compound subject is always **plural** because **all** the subjects are related to the predicate. The time-oriented verb form or aux-word must agree with this plural subject. (Agreement is also discussed in Chapter 4, section 2 and Chapter 5, section 2.)

Basic Sentences	Subjects	Predicate	Combined
Max works in a mine. Mike works in a mine.	Max Mike	works in a mine.	Max and Mike *work* in a mine.

Or indicates a **choice** of subjects. When *or* is used the resulting compound subject is either singular or plural, depending on the subject closest to the verb.

> Bob *or* the girls *are* coming tomorrow.
> The girls *or* Bob is coming tomorrow.

To emphasize the fact that a choice is being made, use *either...or....* To add negative emphasis, use *neither...nor....*

> Either Bob or the girls are coming. (I can't remember who.)
> Neither Bob nor the girls are coming. (Nobody is coming.)

When **more than two subjects** are combined by compounding, commas are placed between them. The word *and* or *or* is placed only between the last two in the series.

Basic Sentences	Subjects	Predicate	Combined
Trees need sunlight. Flowers need sunlight. Grass needs sunlight. All other plants need sunlight.	Trees Flowers Grass All other plants	need sunlight.	*Trees, flowers, grass, and all other plants* need sunlight.

Basic Sentences	Subjects	Predicate	Combined
Joe borrowed my car. Charlie borrowed my car. Somebody else borrowed my car.	Joe Charlie Somebody else	borrowed my car.	*Joe, Charlie, or somebody else* borrowed my car.

1.3   When two or more sentences have the **same subject** but **different predicates**, the predicates may be compounded by using the words *and, or,* or *but*. This compounding process results in one sentence.

But is used to show a **contrast** between the compounded parts.

Basic Sentences	Combined
Sharks live in water. Sharks breathe with gills. Sharks do not have scales.	Sharks live in water and breathe with gills. Sharks live in water but don't have scales. Sharks live in water and breathe with gills but don't have scales.

1.4   When related sentences have other parts which are identical, the identical parts are used only once when the sentences are combined by compounding. The **different** parts must be repeated and connected with *and, or,* or *but*.

Compound objects

	Subject	Verb	Objects	Combined
Joe raises *cows.* Joe raises *sheep.*	Joe	raises	cows. sheep.	Joe raises *cows and sheep.*

Compound complements of the same kind (e.g., all adjectives)

	Subject	*be*-aux	Complements	Combined
Susie is *tall.* Susie is *thin.* Susie is *good-looking.*	Susie	is	tall. thin. good-looking.	Susie is *tall, thin,* and *good-looking.*

Compound shifters of the same category (e.g., time shifters. Categories of shifters are discussed in Chapter 7, section 3.)

	Shifter	Sentence	Combined
In the morning, Joe milks cows. *Every night,* Joe milks cows.	In the morning, Every night,	Joe milks cows.	*In the morning and every night,* Joe milks cows.

Verb forms following the same aux-word

	Subject	**Aux**	**Verb form, etc.**	**Combined**
Stella **is** *studying.* Stella **is** *learning.*	Stella	is	studying. learning.	Stella **is** *studying and learning.*
The plant **may** *grow.* The plant **may** *die.*	The plant	may	grow. die.	The plant **may** *grow or die.*
Bill **has** *done the work.* Bill **has** *passed the class.*	Bill	has	done the work. passed the class.	Bill **has** *done the work and passed the class.*

Nouns following the same article

	Sentence	**Article**	**Noun**	**Combined**
My sister bought **a** *dress.* My sister bought **a** *coat.* My sister bought **a** *hat.*	My sister bought	a	dress. coat. hat	My sister bought **a** *dress, coat, and hat.*
The repairman fixed **the** *washer.* The repairman fixed **the** *refrigerator.*	The repairman fixed	the	washer. refrigerator.	The repairman fixed **the** *washer and refrigerator.*

Adjectives of the same class

	Sentence	**Adjectives**	**(Object)**	**Combined**
Voters elect *city officials.* Voters elect *county officials.* Voters elect *state officials.* Voters elect *national officials.*	Voters elect	city county state national	officials.	Voters elect *city, county, state, and national officials.*

Note that in all the above examples of compounding, the parts that are not repeated (not compounded) are **exactly** the same.

1.5   Sentence parts that are compounded must belong to the same category or class. In other words, they must be parallel.

Parallel construction (an important feature of correct, grammatical writing) means that compounded parts belong to the same category **and** have a meaningful relationship. For example, even though the subjects of the sentences below are the same, the complements **cannot** be compounded.

Simple	**Subject**	*be-*aux.	**Complement**	**Combined**
John's father is *a banker.* John's father is *handsome.* John's father is *at home.*	John's father	is	a banker (noun) handsome (adjective) at home (prep. phrase)	Compounding is NOT POSSIBLE.

There are two reasons why they cannot be compounded:

1. the complements are not of the same kind (one is a noun, one is an adjective, and one is a prepositional phrase), and
2. there is no meaningful relationship between *banker, handsome,* and *at home.*

EXERCISE 1-A

Combine sentences in the groups below by using compound subjects, compound predicates, and other compounds. (If there is only one sentence after a number, leave it uncombined.) Then write all the sentences in paragraph form.

EATING STYLES

1. Some people believe that the way a person eats reveals his personality.

2. Some people eat heartily.

3. They sit down at the table.
   They gobble up everything within reach.

4. Others eat fastidiously.

5. They sit down at the table.
   They pick up each piece of food carefully.
   They examine it for a moment.
   They finally eat it.

6. A few eaters eat in a mixed-up way.

7. They mix up different kinds of food on their plates.
   They don't mind eating mixed food.

8. They eat gravy in one bite.
   They eat peas in one bite.
   They eat meat in one bite.
   They eat salad in one bite.

9. The opposite style of eating is to keep everything separate.

10. Some people don't like everything all mixed up.
    Some people eat in a very organized fashion.

11. They start with their vegetable.
    They finish it before starting their meat.

12. Others rotate their food.

13. They take one bite of one kind of food.
    They take a second bite of another kind of food.
    They take a third bite of a third kind of food.
    They then start the cycle again.

EXERCISE 1-B

Combine sentences in the groups below by using compound subjects, compound predicates, and other compounds. (If there is only one sentence after a number, leave it uncombined.) Then write all the sentences in paragraph form.

A WESTERN

1. Would you like to write a western story?
   Would you like to write a western novel?

2. It's not difficult.

3. All it takes is time and imagination.

4. First you'll need a pad of paper.
   First you'll need a pencil.
   First you'll need a place to write.

5. Next decide on the kind of story.
   Next decide on its location.

6. Your hero should be poor.
   Your hero should be honest.
   Your hero should be suspected by the heroine's father.
   Your hero should be possibly suspected by the reader.

7. The heroine must be beautiful.
   The heroine must be secretly in love with the hero.
   The heroine must be willing to sacrifice herself.
   The heroine must be willing to sacrifice her happiness to save her father and the ranch.

8. The villain will desire the girl.
   The villain will desire the gold mine.
   The villain will desire the ranch.
   The villain always wants to destroy the hero.

9. He should be willing to lie.
   He should be willing to cheat.
   He should be willing to kill to get what he wants.

10. At the story's end, right must prevail.
    At the story's end, the hero must rescue the girl.
    At the story's end, the hero must win her father's gratitude.

EXERCISE 1-C   *Combine sentences in the groups below by using compound subjects, compound predicates, and other compounds. (If there is only one sentence after a number, leave it uncombined.) Then write all the sentences in paragraph form.*

HOUSES

1. People all over the world build houses.
   People all over the world like their homes.

2. Houses are built in many shapes.
   Houses are built in many sizes.

3. Houses are built of grass.
   Houses are built of palm leaves.
   Houses are built of wood.
   Houses are built of steel.
   Houses are built of stone.
   Houses are built of adobe.
   Houses are built of brick.
   Houses are built of plaster.
   Houses are built of concrete.
   Houses are built of other materials.

4. The construction may be simple.
   The construction may be complex.

5. Construction must be adapted to the climate.
   Construction must be adapted to the materials available.
   Construction must be adapted to the skills of the workers.

2. Compounding Sentences

2.1   Even sentences with no identical parts may be compounded **if** (and only if) they are related. When sentences are compounded, each sentence has equal weight. One is not more important than another.

The following words may be used to combine sentences by compounding:

and   (shows coordination)

> I work as a carpenter, **and** my brother assists me.

or (shows choice)

> He will come to my house, **or** I will go to his for the holidays.

but (indicates contrast)

> I plan to major in psychology, **but** I may change my mind.

yet (indicates contrast)

> Bananas won't grow in cold places, **yet** apples need cold weather.

so (shows purpose or reason)

> The students wanted to pass the course, **so** they studied hard.

for (shows cause or reason)

> No one could get into town, **for** the roads were blocked.

nor (used only with compounded *negative* sentences. It is the negative counterpart of *and. Nor* means *and neither.* In the second compounded sentence, the negative marker is included in the word *nor*, and the aux-word must be placed in front of the subject, as in yes/no questions.)

> Matilda can't sing, **nor** *can she* play the piano.
> Joseph won't go, **nor** *will he* support us.

; (can be used to compound two *closely related* short sentences. A semicolon does not indicate any relationship in addition to the relationship expressed by the meaning of the basic sentences. The semicolon is also used between sets in a series when there are commas in the sets.)

> I never loved her; I never will.

When used for compounding, all of the words (*and, or, but, yet, so, for,* and *nor*) are called **coordinating conjunctions**.

2.2 Two sentences **cannot** be joined together with **only a comma**. One of the above conjunctions must be used. The result of combining two sentences with only a comma is called a **comma splice**, a common error in written English.

> **Wrong** → They went downtown, we saw them there.
> **Wrong** → Some animals are beautiful, others are ugly.

EXERCISE 2-A   *Write the following sentences in paragraph form, combining the sentences as indicated by the numbered groups and using appropriate conjunctions.*

THE SABER-TOOTH TIGER

1. There are many different kinds of cats.

2. Some of them are tame.
Others are very wild.

3. Some wild cats lived in earlier days.
They are not found on the earth today.

4. Among these is the saber-tooth tiger.

5. It was about the size of the present-day tiger.
Its body was heavier.

6. The saber-tooth tiger had two eight-inch-long upper teeth.
Its name came from these teeth.

7. No one in modern times has ever seen this tiger.
Men have reconstructed its appearance from bones found in tar pits.

EXERCISE 2-B   *Write the following sentences in paragraph form, combining the sentences as indicated by the numbered groups and using appropriate conjunctions.*

CHAMPION ANIMALS

1. Many animals hold records.

2. For example, cheetahs are the animal kingdom's fastest runners.

3. A cheetah can run seventy miles per hour.
It cannot run that fast for more than a few hundred yards.

4. In contrast, the fastest wild dogs and foxes can run around forty miles per hour.
They can keep that speed up for quite a long time.

5. Most snakes cannot go very fast.
The black mamba snake can go twenty miles per hour.

6. Some animals hold records for being slow—even at their fastest.

7. The maximum speed of a giant tortoise is 0.17 miles per hour.
A three-toed sloth moves at about the same speed.

8. Some animals hold records for longevity.

9. One domestic dog lived for twenty years.
A domestic cat lived twenty-eight years.

10. Horses live an average of twenty years.
One horse lived forty-six years!

EXERCISE 2-C   *Write the following sentences in paragraph form, combining the sentences as indicated by the numbered groups and using appropriate conjunctions.*

SOUND

1. Sound must have some material to pass through.
It cannot travel through a vacuum.

2. Sound can travel through a variety of materials.
It travels at different speeds through different mediums.

3. Sound travels through dry air at about 700 miles an hour.
   This is about the speed of a bullet fired from a rifle.

4. Sound goes about 2800 miles an hour through water.
   It moves faster than this through the ground.

5. Sound goes quite rapidly through air.
   It travels faster through solids and liquids.

EXERCISE 2.1-A   *Select related sentences from those below and combine them by compounding. You may compound whole sentences, subjects, predicates, or other parts of sentences. You may also make some sentences into single-word adjectives. All of the sentences do not need to be combined. Some may be left uncombined. When you have finished, rewrite all your sentences (combined and uncombined) in paragraph form.*

LIVING THINGS

All living things need food.

All living things need water.

Some places have a mild climate.

Some places have an abundance of food.

Some places have an abundance of water.

Other places have a very harsh climate.

Other places are very dry.

Other places are very hot.

Other places are very cold.

Other places are icy.

People can travel in search of food.

People can travel in search of water.

Animals can travel in search of food.

Animals can travel in search of water.

Insects can travel in search of food.

Insects can travel in search of water.

Plants cannot travel and look for life's necessities.

They must adapt in order to survive.

Some have adapted very successfully.

Some plants manage to live in hot places.

Some plants manage to live in dry places.

People cannot live very long in deserts without outside aid.

Some plants manage to live in cold places.

Some plants manage to live in icy places.

People cannot live very long in arctic wastelands without outside aid.

EXERCISE 2.1-B   *Select related sentences from those below and combine them by compounding. You may compound whole sentences, subjects, predicates, or other parts of sentences. You may also make some sentences into single-word adjectives. All of the sentences do not need to be combined. Some may be left uncombined. When you have finished, rewrite all your sentences (combined and uncombined) in paragraph form.*

ROPE

Rope making was important in ancient times.

Rope making is important today.

At one time rope was made only by hand.

Today rope is made by hand.

Today rope is made by machines.

In ancient Egypt rope was made from camel hair.

In ancient Egypt rope was made from twisted grass.

In ancient Egypt rope was made from thin copper wire.

Today rope is made from plant fibers.

Today rope is made from metal.

Today rope is made from synthetic fibers.

In ancient Egypt rope was used for tying animals.

In ancient Egypt rope was used for getting water from deep wells.

In ancient Egypt rope was used for pulling large stones.

Today rope is used for many of the same purposes.

Today rope is used for many different purposes.

Today rope is used to support bridges.

Today rope is used to tie things.

Today rope is used to tow vehicles.

Today rope is used to lasso animals.

Today rope is used in construction work.

Today rope is used in many other trades.

Rope is used by campers.

Rope is used by mountain climbers.

We would have a hard time getting along without it.

EXERCISE 2.1-C *Select related sentences from those below and combine them by compounding. You may compound whole sentences, subjects, predicates, or other parts of sentences. You may also make some sentences into single-word adjectives. All of the sentences do not need to be combined. Some may be left uncombined. When you have finished, rewrite all your sentences (combined and uncombined) in paragraph form.*

A NEW KNOT

Sailors have invented knots.

Ropemakers have invented knots.

Hobbyists have invented knots.

They invented over 4,000 separate knots.

New knots are very rare.

The last new knot was invented in 1958.

It was named the Tarbuck knot.

Now, Dr. Edward Hunter has invented a new knot.

Hunter was doodling with some string.

He put two ends opposite each other.

He made a loop in each of them.

Then he pulled them through.

He liked the resulting knot because it was symmetrical.

He liked the resulting knot because it was easy to tie.

Hunter invented the knot over twenty years ago.

He didn't have it appraised until recently.

A knot consultant checked it against examples in seaman's manuals dating back three centuries.

There was nothing like it.

3. Aux-Words as Predicate Substitutes

3.1 When two sentences with similar predicates are combined, the second predicate may sometimes be shortened. This shortening process uses aux-words to take the place of verbs and other parts of the second predicate in much the same way pronouns take the place of previously mentioned noun phrases (explained in Chapter 3).

When an aux-word is used in the predicate, the same aux-word is repeated and the rest of the predicate is deleted. (If there is a multiple aux-word, only the first one is retained.)

When a time-oriented verb is used, the hidden aux-word (explained in Chapter 4, section 5) must be used and the rest of the predicate is deleted.

Basic Sentences	Combined
John doesn't smoke cigarettes. I don't smoke cigarettes.	John doesn't smoke cigarettes, and I don't either. John doesn't smoke cigarettes, and neither do I.
John goes jogging every day. I go jogging every day.	John goes jogging every day, and I do too. John goes jogging every day, and so do I.

3.2 As the above examples show, there are two different ways that the aux-words are used. In one (Method A), the aux-word follows the subject. In the other (Method B), normal word order is *reversed* and the aux-word comes before the subject. The method depends on the conjunctions that are used.

Method A (normal order):

With the following conjunctions, **normal subject and aux-word order** is used.

Conjunctions	Combinations	Examples
and...too	both affirmative sentences	He works hard, and *I do* too.
or	both affirmative sentences	He works hard, or *I do.*
either...or	both affirmative sentences	Either he works hard, or *I do.*
and...either	both negative sentences	He doesn't work hard, and *I don't* either.
but	one affirmative and one negative sentence	He doesn't work hard, but *I do.*
yet	one affirmative and one negative sentence	He works hard, yet *I don't.*
so (showing cause)	any of the above three combinations	He works hard, so *I do* too. He doesn't work hard, so *I don't* (either). He doesn't work hard, so *I do.* He works hard, so *I don't.*

Method B (reverse order):
With the following conjunctions, the **aux-word comes before the subject**.

Conjunctions	Combinations	Examples
and so	both affirmative sentences	He works hard, and so *do I.*
and neither	both negative sentences	He doesn't work hard, and neither *do I.*
nor	both negative sentences	He doesn't work hard, nor *do I.*

Reverse order is **not** used when one sentence is **affirmative** and the other is **negative**.

Note that the negative in the last two example sentences is carried in *neither* or *nor*; therefore, only an affirmative aux-word is used in the second part of the sentence.

EXERCISE 3-A   *Combine the following sentences using both methods A and B whenever possible. If one method is not possible, write* not possible *after the letter. The first one has been done for you.*

ANIMAL EYES

1. Some animals have a complex eye structure.
   Other animals do not have a complex eye structure.

   A. *Some animals have a complex eye structure, but other animals don't.*

   B. *Not possible.*

2. The night-crawling earthworm is eyeless.
   Most other animals aren't eyeless.

   A.

   B.

3. Some animals can't see well in the dark.
Other animals can see well in the dark.

A.

B.

4. Night hunting owls have enormous eyes.
The tarsier, a cousin of the monkey, has enormous eyes.

A.

B.

5. A flying squirrel has large eyes also.
The mole rat doesn't have large eyes.

A.

B.

6. Chameleons have independent swivel eyes.
Most animals don't have independent swivel eyes.

A.

B.

7. Many animals' eyes can't reflect light.
A cat's eyes can reflect light.

A.

B.

8. A hawk's eyes outweigh its brain.
An eagle's eyes outweigh its brain.

A.

B.

9. Moles live in almost complete darkness.
Shrews live in almost complete darkness.

A.

B.

10. Most mollusks don't have two rows of eyes.
A scallop has two rows of eyes.

A.

B.

11. Some animals have compound eyes.
Others don't have compound eyes.

A.

B.

12. Cats can see well in both the light and the dark.
Geckos can see well in both the light and the dark.

A.

B.

13. Most fish don't have eyes that can see up and down at the same time.
    One special tropical fish has eyes that can see up and down at the same time.

    A.

    B.

EXERCISE 3-B   *Combine the following sentences using both methods A and B whenever possible. If one method is not possible, write* not possible *after the letter.*

FISH BAIT

1. Salt water fishermen use bait.
   Fresh water fishermen use bait.

   A.

   B.

2. Some fishermen use live bait when fishing.
   Other fishermen don't use live bait when fishing.

   A.

   B.

3. Live bait consists of insects, worms, and fish.
   Plastic bait consists of insects, worms, and fish.

   A.

   B.

4. Fresh bait isn't expensive.
   Plastic bait is expensive.

   A.

   B.

5. Some fishermen use plastic lures.
   Others do not use plastic lures.

   A.

   B.

6. Fresh bait doesn't last for more than one good strike.
   Plastic bait lasts for more than one good strike.

   A.

   B.

7. Live bait moves by itself.
   Plastic bait doesn't move by itself.

   A.

   B.

8. Using live bait doesn't require lots of practice.
   Using plastic bait requires lots of practice.

   A.

   B.

9. A plastic lure has to be moved very slowly.
   Live bait doesn't have to be moved very slowly.

   A.

   B.

10. Plastic bait has to be jerked at just the right time to catch large game fish.
    Live bait has to be jerked at just the right time to catch large game fish.

    A.

    B.

11. Some fishermen have changed to using plastic lures.
    Others haven't changed to using plastic lures.

    A.

    B.

EXERCISE 3-C

Combine the following sentences using both methods A and B whenever possible. If one method is not possible, write not possible *after the letter.*

THE ARMADILLO

1. The armadillo has traveled a great distance from its traditional home in South America.
   Other wild animals have traveled a great distance from their traditional homes in South America.

   A.

   B.

2. Most of these wild animals are struggling for survival.
   The armadillo isn't struggling for survival.

   A.

   B.

3. This wild animal is flourishing throughout the United States.
   Other wild animals aren't flourishing throughout the United States.

   A.

   B.

4. Most wild animals don't like cleared land.
   The armadillo likes cleared land.

   A.

   B.

5. The armadillo likes fruit and vegetables.
   Some other wild animals don't like fruits and vegetables.

   A.

   B.

6. Most animals have some sort of defense mechanism.
   The armadillo has some sort of defense mechanism.

   A.

   B.

7. The armadillo has sharp claws.
   Some other animals have sharp claws.

   A.

   B.

8. A frightened armadillo can bury itself in hard dirt in about a minute.
   Most other animals can't bury themselves in hard dirt in about a minute.

   A.

   B.

9. The armadillo has bony plates in its upper body skin.
   Some other animals have bony plates in their skin.

   A.

   B.

10. An armadillo can curl itself into a ball, completely covered by its "armor."
    Most other animals with bony plates in their skin can't curl themselves into a ball, completely covered by their armor.

    A.

    B.

11. Some wild animals can't live in ice and snow.
    The armadillo can't live in ice and snow.

    A.

    B.

12. The cold areas of the United States are safe from the pesky armadillo.
    Other areas of the United States aren't safe from the pesky armadillo.

    A.

    B.

EXERCISE 3.1-A   *Select related sentences from those below and combine them. (All of the sentences do not need to be combined.) Then rewrite the entire passage in paragraph form.*

CARVING

Carving is an ancient art.

Carving is still popular today.

Bone is a popular material for carving.

Wood is a popular material for carving.

Stone is difficult to carve.

Items carved from stone last a long time.

Some carved items are useful.

Others are ornamental.

Some carved items are both useful and ornamental.

Some carved items are very large.

Others are very small.

Most countries have distinctive styles of carving.

Most ethnic groups have distinctive styles of carving.

Some people collect carvings of animals.

Others collect different kinds of carvings.

Popular carved items are bowls.

Popular carved items are mugs.

Popular carved items are figurines.

Popular carved items are knives.

EXERCISE 3.1-B   *Select related sentences from those below and combine them. (All of the sentences do not need to be combined.) Then rewrite the entire passage in paragraph form.*

PIGS: INTELLIGENCE AND COURAGE

For many centuries, most people have enjoyed eating pigs.

Most people have not appreciated pigs' other qualities.

A pig's sense of smell is keener than a dog's.

In France, pigs are trained to find truffles growing deep underground by smelling them.

Cats are smart animals.

Dogs are smart animals.

Horses are smart animals.

Pigs are smarter than all three of these animals.

Pigs are the smartest animals in the barnyard.

You can fool a horse with an empty bucket.

You can't fool a pig with an empty bucket.

Pigs are intelligent animals.

Pigs arrive at solutions to problems by thinking them through.

Pigs make decisions by balancing pleasure against pain.

Pigs learn through experience.

Pigs learn through observation.

One sow in England watched hunting dogs perform.

One sow in England learned to be a good "bird dog."

Pigs are courageous.

One brave mother pig protected her young piglets.

One brave mother pig fought off a full grown bear.

One pig was trained to guard a garden plot growing marijuana.

This pig kept investigating police at bay for nearly an hour.

EXERCISE 3.1-C   *Select related sentences from those below and combine them. (All of the sentences do not need to be combined.) Then rewrite the entire passage in paragraph form.*

SPIDER WEBS

Spiders are found all over the world.

They are very shy creatures.

They are very small creatures.

We often don't see them.

We do see their webs.

Spider webs are found on grass blades.

Spider webs are found on bushes.

Spider webs are found in the corners of rooms.

They are not spiders' homes.

They are used for many purposes.

Spiders use them as signal lines.

Spiders use them as traps.

Spiders use them as roads.

Spiders use them as nurseries.

Spider webs are made of different kinds of silk.

Some silk is hard.

Some silk is dry.

Some silk is strong.

It is used for making the framework of the spider's web.

Other silk is fine.

Other silk is sticky.

It is used for trapping insects in the web.

Another type of strong silk is used to make egg cases.

These "baskets" are tough.

These "baskets" are windproof.

These "baskets" are waterproof.

They protect the eggs until they hatch.

Some silk is used for traveling.

To get away from home, a baby spider climbs to a high place.

It faces the wind.

It spins out two or three feet of ballooning silk.

The wind catches the silk.

The wind carries the spider far away.

Spiders are truly fascinating.

Their webs are truly fascinating.

EXERCISE 3.2-A   *Write at least twenty basic sentences on the topic* **books**. *On another sheet of paper combine the related sentences using the methods you have learned so far.*

EXERCISE 3.2-B   *Write at least twenty basic sentences on the topic* **money**. *On another sheet of paper combine the related sentences using the methods you have learned so far.*

EXERCISE 3.2-C   *Write at least twenty basic sentences on the topic* **exercise**. *On another sheet of paper combine the related sentences using the methods you have learned so far.*

10

Passive and Indirect Object Transformations

This chapter will help you combine and transform simple sentences correctly while avoiding or correcting mistakes like these:

- The package was deliver___ on time.
- If anybody breaks the rules, he must be punish___.
- All students must <u>be</u> study hard.
- Computer piracy <u>is usually occurred</u> during transactions with automatic teller machines.
- Everything <u>was happened</u> very fast.
- The basket ___ made of leaves from a coconut palm.
- Albert gave <u>to</u> me the envelope.
- Whenever we receive a letter from my grandmother, my mother reads it ___ us.
- Professor Simmons answered <u>me</u> the question.

44

1. The Passive Transformation

1.1   In modern English, syntax (word order) is very important because much meaning depends on word order. For instance, the two example sentences below use exactly the same words, but their meanings are very different because the order of the words is different.

> The hunter killed the bear.
> The bear killed the hunter.

1.2   Basic sentences that follow normal word order (explained in Chapter 7) are sometimes called **active** constructions. Active constructions are used when the subject of the sentence is necessary to the message being communicated and the writer wants to make it important by putting it at the front of the sentence.

1.3   The **passive** transformation is used for any of the following reasons:

1. The writer wants to **emphasize the object** of the basic sentence (i.e., the object is more important than the subject).

> The toxic chemicals polluted the river.
> (active construction—the chemicals are most important)
>
> The river was polluted by the toxic chemicals.
> (passive construction—the river is most important)

2. The writer wants to **move the subject** of the basic sentence toward the end of the sentence for some reason, such as to place a relative clause (explained in Chapter 12) after it.

> When Mr. Burbank died, his only son inherited the property.
> (active construction)
>
> When Mr. Burbank died, the property was inherited by his only son, who promptly sold it and went on an extended vacation to Europe.
> (passive construction with relative clause at the end)

Putting the subject at the end of the sentence this way avoids overloading the front of the sentence with modifiers when the writer desires to describe the subject in detail.

> At the reception, Mrs. Jeffrey Butler accompanied Mrs. Gray.
> (active construction)
>
> At the reception, Mrs. Gray was accompanied by her sister-in-law, Mrs. Jeffrey Butler, who wore an elegant empire gown of white lace and carried a bouquet of cream-colored chrysanthemums.
> (passive construction with extensive modification at the end)

3. The **subject** (of the basic sentence) **is unimportant or unnecessary** to what is being written. In this case, the *by* + original subject phrase can be omitted.

> A postal worker delivered the mail on time.
> (active construction—but the subject of this sentence is not really important. After all, who else besides a postal worker would deliver the mail?)
>
> The mail was delivered on time.
> (passive construction—since the postal worker is not important, that part of the sentence has been left out.)

4. The **subject** (of the basic sentence) **is not known.**

> Somebody stole Jane's purse.
> (active construction—We don't know who the thief was.)
>
> Jane's purse was stolen.
> (passive construction—The focus is on the robbery, not the unknown robber.)

1.4   Only pattern no. 1 sentences (sentences with objects—explained in Chapter 7) can be transformed from the active to the passive construction.

1.5   The passive sentence transformation follows these ten steps:

> In 1966, two lions attacked my uncle. (active contruction)

Step 1.   Find the simple, basic sentence. Remove any shifters.

> Two lions attacked my uncle.

Step 2.   Locate the object of the sentence. (If there is no object you cannot produce a correct passive construction.)

> Two lions attacked *my uncle*.
> (subject)   (verb)   (object)

Step 3.   Decide if the object should be emphasized more than the subject or if there is any other reason for putting it first in the sentence (variety, parallelism). (If our example sentence is part of a story about *my uncle*, then it will probably be better to use a passive construction and emphasize *him*, and not the lions.)

If there is no reason for using a passive construction then *do not* use it. Too many passive constructions can ruin otherwise good writing. If there is a reason for using a passive construction, then go ahead with the following steps.

Step 4.   Write the *object* of the active construction as the *subject* of the new passive construction. If the object is a pronoun you will have to change it to its subjective form.

> My uncle . . .

Step 5. If there is an aux-word or aux-words (except *didn't* and *don't*) in the active construction, use the same one(s) in the passive construction. BE CAREFUL! If the aux-word is *has, have, is, am, are, was, were,* or one of the negative forms of these aux-words, you may have to change it so that it will agree with the new subject. If the aux-word is *do, does,* or *did,* it must be removed. The same time is preserved by using the appropriate form of *be* in Step 6. If the aux-word is *don't, doesn't,* or *didn't,* the first part must be removed, but the negative marker *not* remains. Any adverbs remain in the same position. If there is no aux-word, then skip this step.

> No aux-word in this example sentence

Step 6. Determine the verb form used in the active construction and write the same form (past or present) of *be* in the new passive sentence. Once again, be careful with agreement. The form of *be* must agree with the new subject (the old object), so you may have to change it from a +*s* form to a no-*s* form or vice versa.

> My uncle *was* (past form of *be* that agrees with the new singular subject) . . .

Step 7. Next, write the *d-t-n* form of the verb that was used in the active construction.

> My uncle was *attacked* (*d-t-n* form of *attack*) . . .

Step 8. Now write the word *by* and then the old (active construction) subject. If the old subject is a pronoun you will have to change it to its objective form.

> My uncle was attacked *by two lions* . . .

Step 9. Determine if this agent (what you just added in Step 8, the word *by* plus the old subject) is necessary or desirable. If it is, then leave it in. If it isn't, then take it out.

> My uncle was attacked *by two lions.* (IN)
> My uncle was attacked. (OUT)

Step 10. Any shifters will remain the same. Put them back in the sentence now.

> *In 1966,* my uncle was attacked by two lions.

Here is another example of the passive transformation. (The instructions have been simplified.)

They were observing her through the window. (active construction)

1. They were observing her. (remove shifter)
2. They were observing *her*. (locate object)
3. Decide if the object should be placed first. (This depends on a number of factors which are not included in these directions.)
4. *She* . . . (New subject, note that the object pronoun *her* has been changed to the subject pronoun *she*)
5. She *was* . . . (aux-word *were* changed to *was* to agree with the new singular subject)
6. She was *being* . . . (*-ing* form of *be* used because *observing* is the *-ing* form)
7. She was being *observed* . . . (*d-t-n* form of active construction verb *observe*)
8. She was being observed *by them*. (new object, note that the subject pronoun *they* has been changed to the object pronoun *them*)
9. She was being observed. (Decide if agent *by them* is important to the meaning of the sentence. In this example it has been left out.)
10. She was being observed *through the window*. (restore shifter)

1.6   An active to passive transformation is *not* possible with all verb meanings. When active-construction sentences containing certain verbs are transformed to the passive, the meaning of the verb changes and/or is unacceptable.

Joyce married Bill last week.
  (meaning change) Bill was married by Joyce last week.

The priest married Joyce and Bill.
  (no meaning change) Joyce and Bill were married by the priest.

Note that *marry* has two different meanings in the above sentences.

The shoe fits her foot perfectly.
  (unacceptable) Her foot is fitted by the shoe perfectly.

The salesman fit the shoe to her foot.
  (acceptable) The shoe was fitted to her foot by the salesman.

Note that *fit* has two different meanings in the above sentences.

EXERCISE 1-A   *Change the following active sentences into passive constructions. With some sentences the passive construction is not possible. Do not change those sentences.*

TIDAL ENERGY

1. The ocean creates tremendous unused energy.

2. The pull of the moon's gravity on the earth's water causes tides.

3. The ocean tides could be man's greatest source of power.

4. The contour of the shoreline frequently determines the size of the tides.

5. In some parts of the world, scientists have measured tides as high as forty feet.

6. Oceanographers can accurately predict the height and time of the tides anywhere on earth.

7. Producing energy from ocean tides does not cause pollution problems.

8. So far, however, man has not harnessed these tides.

9. Modern technicians have met most of man's technological challenges.

10. Mankind should also use the tides' untapped energy.

EXERCISE 1-B   *Change the following active sentences into passive constructions. With some sentences the passive construction is not possible. Do not change those sentences.*

CAMOUFLAGE

1. Humans and animals have always used camouflage as a protection against their enemies.

2. Humans have decorated or painted warships, ammunition dumps, and soldiers' helmets to conceal them from enemy eyes.

3. However, nature has produced the best camouflage in the world.

4. Brilliantly colored tropical fish hide in the brightly colored coral reefs of the ocean.

5. The white arctic wastes hide the polar bear and the snowy owl.

6. The spotted fawn blends into its forest background.

7. Humans have adapted many of nature's techniques in the search for camouflage.

8. Humans have developed camouflage clothing.

9. Soldiers camouflage equipment to prevent the enemy from seeing it.

10. At the present time, human camouflage methods are not equal to nature's methods.

EXERCISE 1-C   *Change the following active sentences into passive construction. With some sentences the passive construction is not possible. Do not change those sentences.*

HAZARDOUS HABITS

1. Liquor and tobacco bring on much misery and destruction.

2. Drinking drivers cause well over half of the automobile accidents in the United States.

3. Drinking problems ruin many families.

4. A mother's use of liquor and/or tobacco affects unborn children.

5. Millions of Americans use tobacco.

6. Tobacco can cause heart trouble and cancer.

7. Carelessly discarded cigarettes cause many destructive fires.

8. Advertisers must print a health hazard warning on all advertising for cigarettes.

9. The manufacturers also print this warning on every package of cigarettes.

10. Perhaps someday, people will wake up to the dangers of hazardous habits.

2. Overuse of the Passive Construction

Do not overuse the passive. A common mistake is to use too many passive constructions when writing. (Some people think that using passive construction sentences makes their writing sound "distinguished." This is not true.) For this reason, it may sometimes be necessary for you to change passive constructions to active constructions.

When a passive construction without an agent (the original subject of the active sentence) is changed to an active construction, the writer must supply the subject (which may have been stated previously or is understood).

EXERCISE 2-A

Find the passive constructions below and change them from the passive to the active construction. In some sentences it may be necessary to supply the subject and/or change the pronouns.

A FOOTBALL GAME

1. Football is played by many young people.

2. The game is begun by a kick off.

3. The ball is run back by a receiver.

4. Sometimes the ball is run all the way back for a touchdown.

5. The fans' approval is roared.

6. The ball is often passed by the quarterback to one of the ends.

7. Frequently the ball is dropped.

8. Pass interference may be called by a referee.

9. Occasionally the quarterback is sacked by the opposing players for a big loss.

10. The fans are let down when their team fails to win.

EXERCISE 2-B

Find the passive constructions below and change them from the passive to the active construction. In some sentences it may be necessary to supply the subject and/or change the pronouns.

A PARTY

1. The party had been planned by the hostess well in advance.

2. Invitations were sent by her several weeks before the party.

3. They were received by the guests a few days after they were sent.

4. The guests' responses were sent immediately.

5. Final preparations for the party were made.

6. On the night of the party, the guests were welcomed at the door by the hostess.

7. The guests who didn't know each other were introduced.

8. Music was played by a band.

9. Refreshments were served.

10. The party was enjoyed by all who were there.

EXERCISE 2-C   *Find the passive constructions below and change them from the passive to the active construction. In some sentences it may be necessary to supply the subject.*

A GAME-WINNING PLAY

1. The game was being watched by many people.

2. The game was being lost by the home team.

3. The game was being led by the visitors by one point.

4. In the last inning, two batters had been struck out by the visiting team's pitcher.

5. A fast ball was pitched by the pitcher to the third batter.

6. Then, a curve was thrown.

7. The next pitch was hit by the batter.

8. The ball was knocked high and deep into centerfield.

9. The centerfield fence was hit by the ball.

10. It was caught by the centerfielder as it bounced back off the fence.

11. The game was won by that play.

EXERCISE 2.1-A

In the sentences below there are some active constructions that will be better in the passive. Change them (and only them) to passive constructions. Then write all the sentences in paragraph form.

AIR MAIL

1. Today, airplanes and helicopters carry mail through the air.

2. They can carry heavy bags and boxes of mail.

3. They have even flown elephants from India to the United States.

4. Years ago, before people invented airplanes, carrier pigeons delivered air mail.

5. These carrier pigeons carried messages strapped to their legs.

6. These messages had to be very light because the birds were very small.

7. People carried the birds in cages to their destination.

8. They strapped a message in a capsule to the pigeon's leg.

9. When the cages were opened, the birds flew back to their homes.

10. There, they delivered the messages.

EXERCISE 2.1-B

In the sentences below there are some active constructions that will be better in the passive. Change them (and only them) to passive constructions. Then write all the sentences in paragraph form.

SURVIVAL IN THE DESERT

1. Man needs food and water to survive in the desert.

2. The more important of these is water.

3. A person can find water holes by watching the direction birds fly at dawn and at dusk.

4. People can also find water inside barrel cactus plants.

5. One must squeeze or chew the pulp to get the liquid.

6. People also find water in the roots of desert trees.

7. These roots are close to the surface and spread for twenty or thirty feet.

8. A person can also collect dew from the limbs of dead brush.

9. People do this at daybreak by wiping the limbs with a cloth and wringing it out.

10. A person can collect about a quart of water in an hour in the early morning.

EXERCISE 2.1-C   *In the sentences below there are some active constructions that will be better in the passive. Change them (and only them) to passive constructions. Then write all the sentences in paragraph form.*

SOCCER FEVER

1. Not many years ago, almost no one in the United States played soccer.

2. Few people knew even the basic rules of the top sport in the 140 nations.

3. They considered soccer a foreign sport.

4. People in the United States didn't understand other nations' enthusiasm for soccer.

5. Then, in 1974, the New York Cosmos soccer team recruited Pelé, a retired superstar from Brazil.

6. The Brazilian master showed his teammates how to really play soccer.

7. His teammates learned their lessons well.

8. The New York Cosmos won the North American Soccer League championship in 1977.

9. Soccer fever began to sweep the United States.

10. Today millions of American boys and girls play youth soccer.

11. Perhaps someday a team from the United States will win the prestigious World Cup.

3. The Indirect Object Transformation

3.1   The prepositional phrases *to* + **noun phrase** or *for* + **noun phrase** often follow the object of certain verbs in sentence pattern no. 1. If the noun phrase following the *to* or *for* receives the object, then the indirect object transformation may be used.

Sentences like those below can be transformed using the indirect object transformation.

I sold my book to your friend.
I sold your friend my book. (indirect object transformation)

The bride threw her bouquet to Susan.
The bride threw Susan her bouquet. (indirect object transformation)

He bought some candy for the children.
He bought the children some candy. (indirect object transformation)

3.2   There are five steps in the indirect object transformation:

Step 1.   Make sure the sentence has an object of the verb. (sentence pattern no. 1)

He gave *a new coat of paint* to the house.
　　　　　　(object of the verb)

Step 2.   Make sure the verb allows an indirect object transformation (see section 3.3). (*Give* is on the list of verbs which allow the transformation.)

Step 3.   Make sure that the noun following *to* or *for* receives the object of the verb. (It may not be a noun of place.)

He gave a new coat of paint to *the house.*
　　　　　　　　　(receives the new coat of paint)

Step 4.   Move the prepositional phrase (*to* + **noun phrase** or *for* + **noun phrase**) to a new position between the verb and the object of the verb.

> He gave *to the house* a new coat of paint.

(Warning: It is not possible to stop at this stage. This sentence is ungrammatical. You must continue to Step 5.)

Step 5.   Remove the word *to* or *for*.

> He gave *the house* a new coat of paint.
>   (indirect object)

Here is another example sentence with *for* + **noun phrase** instead of a *to* + **noun phrase**. The process is the same.

> **Step 1.**   My grandmother made a *sweater* for my brother. (check for an object of the verb)
>
> **Step 2.**   (*Make* is on the list of verbs that allow the transformation.)
>
> **Step 3.**   My grandmother made a sweater for *my brother*. (my brother received the sweater)
>
> **Step 4.**   My grandmother made *for my brother* a sweater. (move to new position)
>
> **Step 5.**   My grandmother made my brother a sweater. (remove *for*)

3.3   Only pattern no. 1 sentences with certain verbs can be transformed. With some transitive verbs the transformation may be done, but it is not necessary. With other transitive verbs the transformation cannot be done.
Sentences containing the following verbs **may** be transformed.

to + noun phrase		
advance	loan	send
bring	mail	serve
deny	offer	ship
drop	owe	show
end	pass	sing
extend	pay	supply
feed	pitch	take
give	present	teach
grant	promise	tell
hand	read	throw
issue	rent	write
leave	sell	

for + noun phrase		
bake	do	pack
boil	find	paint
build	fry	peel
buy	get	pour
call	leave	quote
catch	light	reserve
cook	make	roast
cut	mix	save
dig	order	sew

Sentences containing the following verbs **cannot** be transformed.

address	explain	repeat
announce	introduce	report
answer	mention	return
cash	open	say
change	prescribe	speak
close	pronounce	suggest
describe	prove	

3.4   With a few verbs, if there is a receiver of the verb's action, the receiver (indirect object) *must* be put before the object of the verb. (It cannot be placed following *to* or *for*.)

> The book cost me a lot of money.
> **unacceptable** → The book cost a lot of money to me.

The following are some of these verbs.

allow	save
ask	trade
charge	wish
cost	

3.5   When the object of the verb in the basic sentence is a **pronoun**, the indirect object tranformation should **not** be done.

> He read the letter to us.
> He read us the letter.
> He read it to us.
> **unacceptable** → He read us it.

EXERCISE 3-A

Some of the sentences below have to + noun *or* for + noun *phrases which can be transformed into indirect objects. When possible, make the transformation. Then rewrite all the sentences in paragraph form.*

BASEBALLS

1. To start the World Series, an invited dignitary throws the first ball to the catcher.

2. The catcher then hands this ball to the special visitor.

3. Many balls are needed for the World Series games.

4. Some balls are ruined by foul tips.

5. Players usually toss these damaged balls to the fans.

6. Batters frequently hit home run balls into the stands.

7. Collectors offer a lot of money for these balls.

8. During the game, the catcher may hand a ball which he thinks is bad to the umpire.

9. The umpire continually throws new balls to the pitcher.

10. When a pitcher is relieved, he hands the ball to the team manager.

11. The team manager, in turn, hands the ball to the new pitcher, and the game continues.

EXERCISE 3-B   *Some of the sentences below have* to + noun *or* for + noun *phrases which can be transformed into indirect objects. When possible, make the transformation. Then rewrite all the sentences in paragraph form.*

TEACHERS AND TESTS

1. Teachers teach lessons to students.

2. Good teachers give all the help they can to their students.

3. They prepare special materials for them to help them learn.

4. After teaching their students, they give tests to them.

5. They don't give tests to punish the students.

6. They give them to evaluate the students' progress.

7. After they have evaluated the students' progress, teachers must give grades to the students.

8. The school sends a grade report to each student.

9. The students are supposed to show it to their parents.

10. In case they don't, the school sends a duplicate of the report to each student's parents also.

EXERCISE 3-C   *Some of the sentences below have* to + noun *or* for + noun *phrases which can be transformed into indirect objects. When possible, make the transformation. Then rewrite all the sentences in paragraph form.*

HALLOWEEN

1. Halloween is a fun holiday for children.

2. Some parents buy costumes for their children.

3. Other parents make costumes for their children.

4. The children go from door to door in the evening.

5. They say, "Trick or treat," to people in their homes.

6. The people give candy to the children.

7. Some parents have parties for their children.

8. They prepare treats for them.

9. They tell scary stories to them.

10. After Halloween, people begin to prepare for Thanksgiving and Christmas.

4. Passive and Indirect Object Transformations Together

4.1   With some verbs and some sentences, both indirect object and passive transformations can be performed (in that order). The indirect object will then become the subject of the passive construction.

They gave an award to Mr. Howard. (basic sentence, active construction)
They gave Mr. Howard an award. (indirect object transformation)
Mr. Howard was given an award. (passive transformation)

The company paid $500 to Karl for that last job. (basic sentence, active construction)
The company paid Karl $500 for that last job. (indirect object transformation)
Karl was paid $500 for that last job. (passive transformation)

My office will send a bill to you next week. (basic sentence, active construction)
My office will send you a bill next week. (indirect object transformation)
You will be sent a bill next week. (passive transformation)

The law firm offered an attractive position to Sally. (basic sentence, active construction)
The law firm offered Sally an attractive position. (indirect object transformation)
Sally was offered an attractive position. (passive transformation)

4.2   Be careful. With some verbs, the use of both transformations together is not possible. The result will be an incorrect sentence.

My grandmother made a sweater for my brother. (basic sentence, active construction)
My grandmother made my brother a sweater. (indirect object transformation)
My brother was made a sweater. (INCORRECT!)

EXERCISE 4-A   *Write a descriptive paragraph about your* **favorite book**. *Use passive constructions and indirect object transformations whenever appropriate. Underline each of them.*

EXERCISE 4-B   *Write a descriptive paragraph about your* **favorite food**. *Use passive constructions and indirect object transformations whenever appropriate. Underline each of them.*

EXERCISE 4-C   *Write a descriptive paragraph about your* **favorite game**. *Use passive constructions and indirect object transformations whenever appropriate. Underline each of them.*

11

Half-Sentences
(Participial Phrases)

This chapter will help you combine simple sentences correctly while avoiding or correcting mistakes like these:

- Being careful about my actions, people respect me more.
- While fishing, the clouds started to get thick and dark.
- I saw a beautiful sunrise going to school this morning.
- It, struggling for breath, crawled out of the water.
- That man driving away in the red car with the big mustache is my uncle.
- We found a dead butterfly walking home from work.
- Realizing that the end of the trip was near and knew that home and food were not far away, the horse found new energy.
- The people were shocked at the rising crime rate, called for the police chief's resignation.

1. Same Subject and Aux-Word *be*

1.1 Another method of combining related sentences is by making one into a half-sentence (often called a *participial phrase* in traditional, Latin-based grammars) and attaching it to the main sentence. This method is used to combine sentences which have the same subject.

> John was walking to school this morning.
> John noticed the cherry trees were blooming.
>
> The breaking waves were whipped by the wind.
> The breaking waves threw spray high into the air.

1.2 A sentence which contains a *be* aux-word (*am, is, are, was, were*, etc.) is made into a half-sentence by dividing the sentence between the aux-word and the verb and removing the first part (the subject and the aux-word).

> John was walking to school this morning.
> John was   /   walking to school this morning.
>   Half-sentence: walking to school this morning.
>
> The breaking waves were whipped by the wind.
> The breaking waves were   /   whipped by the wind.
>   Half-sentence: whipped by the wind.

1.3 A half-sentence is no longer a complete sentence and cannot stand alone. It must be attached to another sentence. This half-sentence is placed either (1) immediately before the subject, or (2) immediately after the nucleus of the subject of the main sentence (unless the subject is a third-person pronoun or unless there are modifying phrases or clauses after the nucleus [explained in Chapter 8]).

> Walking to school this morning, John noticed the cherry trees were
>   blooming.
> John, walking to school this morning, noticed the cherry trees were
>   blooming.
>
> Whipped by the wind, the breaking waves threw spray high into the air.
> The breaking waves, whipped by the wind, threw spray high into the air.

Notice that the half-sentence relates directly to the subject. For this reason the two sentences which are combined using this method must have the same subject. The sentences below should not be combined because the resulting sentence would be incorrect or misleading. (Traditionally, these errors are called *dangling participles*.)

John was walking to school this morning.
The cherry trees were blooming.

incorrect → Walking to school this morning, the cherry trees were blooming. (Cherry trees don't walk to school.)

Roger was sleeping in the library. His class started without him.

incorrect → Sleeping in the library, his class started without him.

EXERCISE 1-A   *If possible, combine each of the following groups of two sentences into one sentence each by making a half-sentence of one of the sentences and then attaching it to the other. (Note: some pairs cannot be combined because the subjects are different.)*

THE GREAT TRAIN ROBBERY

1. The Great Train Robbery of 1885 was an unprecedented crime.
The Great Train Robbery of 1885 occurred in Victorian England.

2. It was called the Crime of the Century.
It involved many people and tremendous planning.

3. Plans for the robbery were well prepared and coordinated.
Plans for the robbery took over a year to perfect.

4. Gold was stolen from safes on the train.
The safes contained gold to pay soliders in the Crimean War.

5. The amount stolen was large but not the largest to date.
The amount stolen appeared less significant than the crime itself.

6. The railroads were considered the hallmark of progress.
The railroads represented the material advancement that would eventually lead to the eradication of crime.

7. Crime was compared to the plague.
Crime would inevitably disappear with changing social conditions.

8. This crime was not linked to social conditions.
This crime came from another source.

9. People were absolutely astonished to discover that crime could prey on progress.
People called this robbery the Crime of the Century.

10. The Great Train Robbery is still remembered over one hundred years after it took place.
The Great Train Robbery captures the attention and imagination of all who read about it.

EXERCISE 1-B   *If possible, combine each of the following groups of two sentences into one sentence each by making a half-sentence of one of the sentences and then attaching it to the other. (Note: some pairs cannot be combined because the subjects are different.)*

THE TAJ MAHAL

1. The Taj Mahal is one of the most beautiful buildings in the world.
The Taj Mahal immortalizes the love of the emperor Shah Jahan for his favorite wife.

2. It was built for the tomb of Mumtaz Mahal.
It has become the symbol of the Eastern world.

3. The building is magnificently proportioned.
The building awes visitors from all over the world.

4. The Taj Mahal must be seen to be appreciated.
Many visitors come at full moon to see it.

5. It rises from a platform with buildings of red sandstone at each side.
It is reflected in a long, rectangular pool.

6. Four famous minarets are judged the most graceful towers in the world.
Four famous minarets surround it.

7. They are crowned with eight-windowed cupolas.
They taper to a majestic height of 138 feet.

8. The Taj Mahal was begun in 1630 and completed in 1648.
The Taj Mahal has remained in excellent condition for about 350 years.

9. An enormous room is inside of the Taj.
An enormous room contains the octagonal burial chamber of Shah Jahan and Mumtaz Mahal.

10. A famous marble screen encircles the coffin.
A famous marble screen is carved in filigree that can only be compared to lace.

11. Mosaics are set with thirty-five kinds of rare stones.
Mosaics decorate the burial chamber in an enormous marble room.

EXERCISE 1-C

If possible, combine each of the following groups of two sentences into one sentence each by making a half-sentence of one of the sentences and then attaching it to the other. (Note: some pairs cannot be combined because the subjects are different.)

CATALOG BUSINESS

1. Mail order catalogs are an important part of American commerce.
Mail order catalogs do millions of dollars of business every year.

2. Mail order catalogs allow people to shop without leaving their homes.
Mail order catalogs are published by many large retail businesses.

3. Several companies are well known because of their catalogs.
Several companies lead all others in catalog sales.

4. Montgomery Ward was started in 1872.
Montgomery Ward was the first large store to sell a variety of goods by mail.

5. Sears, Roebuck and Company was started a few years later, in 1886.
   Sears, Roebuck and Company began selling mail order watches.

6. Millions of Americans were scattered throughout rural America.
   Millions of Americans lived far from large stores that offered a wide selection of goods.

7. These rural Americans were looking for a convenient way to purchase the things they needed.
   These rural Americans eagerly requested their catalogs.

8. Their desires for material goods were fired by the many illustrations the catalogs contained.
   Their desires for material goods increased as they read the descriptions of each item in the catalogs.

9. Sears was ahead of Montgomery Ward in sales volume by 1900.
   Sears has never been in second place since that time.

10. Sears is now more than one hundred years old.
    Sears has expanded its operations to where more is sold in its stores than through its catalogs.

11. Sears is still the biggest publisher in the entire United States.
    Sears publishes well over three hundred million catalogs per year.

12. In some years, Sears, Roebuck and Company has accounted for a full one percent of the gross national product of the entire country.
    Sears, Roebuck and Company is the largest retail business in the United States.

2. Same Subject and Time-Included Verb Form

2.1 A sentence which contains a **time-included verb** is made into a half-sentence by

1. dividing the sentence between the subject and the verb,
2. removing the subject, and then
3. changing the time-included verb form to the timeless *-ing* form.

The half-sentence formed in this way must be added to the main sentence either

immediately **before** the subject, or
immediately **after** the subject of the main sentence.

John walked to school this morning.
John noticed that the cherry trees were blooming.
  Walking to school this morning, John noticed the cherry trees were blooming. (before the subject)
  John, walking to school this morning, noticed the cherry trees were blooming. (after the subject)

3. Same Subject, Aux-Word, and Timeless Verb Form

3.1   A sentence containing the aux-words *will, shall, do, does, did, don't, doesn't,* or *didn't* (followed by the timeless base form of a verb) can also be made into a half-sentence by

1. dividing the sentence between the subject and the verb
2. removing the aux-word
3. changing the base form of the verb to the *-ing* form.

> John will study biology next year.
> John will dissect a frog.
>   Studying biology next year, John will dissect a frog.

If the base form *be* follows these aux-words, it also should be removed.

3.2   When one of the aux-words *don't, doesn't,* or *didn't* or *do, does,* or *did* plus *not* (*do not, does not,* or *did not*) is used, the aux-word is removed but the negative *not* remains.

> John didn't know the answers to the test.
> John failed the test.
>   John, not knowing the answers, failed the test.

3.3   Sentences containing the aux-words *have, has,* or *had* (followed by the timeless *d-t-n* form of the verb) can also be made into half-sentences. In these sentences the aux-word (*have, has,* or *had*) is changed to the timeless *-ing* form *having,* but it still indicates earlier time. The *d-t-n* form of the verb remains.

> John has experienced many serious problems in his life.
> John endures minor discomforts without complaining.
>   Having experienced many serious problems in his life, John endures
>   minor discomforts without complaining.

EXERCISE 3-A   *If possible, combine each of the following groups of two sentences into one sentence each by making a half-sentence of one of the sentences (whichever one works best) and then attaching it to the other.*

CARBOHYDRATES

1. "Simple" carbohydrates constitute many different sugars.
   "Simple" carbohydrates exist in many food products.

2. Sugars consist of one or two small sugar molecules.
Sugars supply quick energy to the body.

3. Cereals, fruits, and even milk contain different kinds of sugar.
Cereals, fruits, and even milk provide the energy our bodies need to stay alive.

4. Table sugar contains sucrose.
Table sugar satisfies a large part of our daily energy needs.

5. Fruits contain a sugar called fructose.
Fruits offer an alternative source of energy.

6. The kind of sugar found in milk is called lactose.
Most people don't even realize that milk contains sugar.

7. Starch and related carbohydrates contain "complex" carbohydrates.
Starch and related carbohydrates exist naturally in vegetables and grains.

8. They differ from simple carbohydrates.
They consist of long chains of sugar molecules chemically bonded together.

9. The body uses complex carbohydrates less rapidly.
The body takes more time to digest complex carbohydrates.

10. The human body needs both "simple" and "complex" carbohydrates.
The human body must get both kinds in order to function as it should.

EXERCISE 3-B   *If possible, combine each of the following groups of two sentences into one sentence each by making a half-sentence of one of the sentences (whichever one works best) and then attaching it to the other.*

A DANGEROUS DRIVE

1. I usually enjoy a drive in the country.
I consider myself a good driver.

2. The experience I had yesterday made me want to never go out on the highway again.
The experience I had yesterday nearly cost me my life.

3. I went for a drive in the country.
I enjoyed the scenery.

   4. A large truck in front of me blocked my view.
      I couldn't see the road ahead very well.

   5. A car approached from the opposite direction.
      A car came around a curve.

   6. Suddenly, a motorcycle pulled out from behind the car.
      A motorcycle accelerated and started to pass the car.

   7. The motorcycle moved to our side of the road.
      The motorcycle came directly toward us.

   8. The motorcycle driver approached the truck and my car at a fantastic speed.
      The motorcycle driver didn't seem to notice us.

   9. The driver of the truck stomped on his brakes.
      He honked his horn and swerved out of the motorcycle's way.

   10. I nearly hit the back of the truck.
      I stopped my car just in time.

   11. The motorcycle driver zoomed past us at a tremendous speed.
      The motorcycle driver didn't even turn back to look at us.

   12. I look back on the experience now.
      I realize that there are many drivers like the one on the motorcycle.

   13. I know that there are nuts like that on the road.
      I hesitate to risk my life driving.

EXERCISE 3-C   *If possible, combine each of the following groups of two sentences into one sentence each by making a half-sentence of one of the sentences (whichever one works best) and then attaching it to the other.*

NORMAN ROCKWELL

   1. Most people in the United States understand little about art or artists.
      Most people in the United States can still recognize and enjoy the artwork of Norman Rockwell.

   2. Rockwell grew up in and around New York City.
      Rockwell discovered and developed his tremendous talent for realistic illustration as a young man.

3. Rockwell sold his first cover illustration to *The Saturday Evening Post* when he was twenty-two years old.
   Rockwell never lacked work after that.

4. Rockwell painted over three hundred cover illustrations for *The Saturday Evening Post*.
   Rockwell's fame grew because of the work he did for that widely circulated magazine.

5. Rockwell took little time off from work.
   Rockwell worked every day of the year except Christmas.

6. Rockwell referred to himself as an illustrator rather than an artist.
   Rockwell didn't try to be a Picasso.

7. Rockwell commented on the subjects he chose to paint.
   Rockwell once said that he painted the world as he wanted it to be.

8. Rockwell's art remains today as a cultural testimony of the times he lived in.
   Rockwell's art depicts many of the social issues which were important in the United States during his lifetime.

9. Rockwell's paintings made him the most famous American illustrator of his era.
   Rockwell's paintings created a portrait of America that millions of people loved.

4. Subject and Object the Same

4.1 When the subject of one sentence is the **object** of another, the half-sentence method of combining may be used. The sentence with the noun in common used as the **subject** always becomes the **half-sentence**. The sentence with the noun in common used as an **object** must be the **main** sentence. The half-sentence **follows the object** of the main sentence. It does not precede it.

> I saw the dog.
> The dog was wagging its tail.
> I saw the dog wagging its tail.

4.2 With some verbs, sentences combined in this way may be ambiguous. They may be confusing to the reader because there are two possible meanings.

> I saw the dog walking down the street.
> (It is not clear who or what was walking down the street, the dog or I.)

When the object of a sentence is the subject of a passive sentence (explained in Chapter 10) and that passive sentence becomes the half-sentence, there is no problem with ambiguity.

Everyone listened to the band.
The band was led by the new director.
   Everyone listened to the band led by the new director.

We always enjoy bread.
Bread is baked by my mother.
   We always enjoy bread baked by my mother.

EXERCISE 4-A   *If possible, combine each of the following groups of two sentences into a single sentence each by making a half-sentence of one of the sentences and then attaching it to the other. Use any of the methods discussed in this chapter.*

THE NOBEL PRIZE

1. Alfred Bernhard Nobel was born in 1833.
   Alfred Bernhard Nobel was a Swedish chemist and inventor.

2. Nobel experimented with nitroglycerine in order to find a safer explosive.
   Nobel perfected a combination of nitroglycerine and diatomaceous earth.
   The combination of nitroglycerine and diatomaceous earth was called dynamite.

3. Nobel was inclined toward pacifism.
   Nobel was unhappy with the use of his inventions.

4. He made a fortune from his inventions.
   He left his money in a funded foundation.

5. The interest from this fund was given as awards.
   The awards were for the promotion of international peace.

6. The Nobel Foundation gives awards for work in physics, chemistry, physiology, medicine, and peacemaking efforts.
   The awards are called Nobel Prizes.

7. A Nobel Prize consists of a gold medal, a sum of money, and a diploma.
   A Nobel Prize is awarded without regard to nationality.

8. The prizes are given on December tenth of each year.
   December tenth is the anniversary of Nobel's death.

EXERCISE 4-B   *If possible, combine each of the following groups of two sentences into a single sentence each by making a half-sentence of one of the sentences and then attaching it to the other. Use any of the methods discussed in this chapter.*

THE COLONIZATION OF SPACE

1. People have many fantastic dreams.
   The dreams concern man's future.

2. One popular idea about the future predicts space colonies.
   The space colonies revolve around the earth.

3. Initially the space colonies will be able to sustain only a few dozen workers at a time.
   The space colonies will eventually expand in size and increase in comfort to the point where up to 50,000 people will live together in space.

4. The space colonies will feature carefully controlled environments for the people who inhabit them.
   The space colonies will be pleasant places to live and work.

5. The colonies' habitats will include swimming pools, artificial rivers, and comfortable apartments.
   The comfortable apartments will overlook pest-free, climate-controlled gardens.

6. They will receive solar energy.
   The solar energy will be reflected toward the colony by huge mirrors.

7. The colonies will be shaped like giant wheels.
   The colonies will spin to produce centrifugal force.
   The centrifugal force will simulate earth's gravity.

8. Many scientists imagine that the space colonies will be mini-utopias.
   Many scientists look forward to these future space colonies.

9. Some critics of this utopian dream point out that this space colony plan does not take into account man's social problems.
   Some critics of this utopian dream say it will never succeed.

10. They look at progress in another way.
    They believe that man should solve the problems of his society on earth instead of simply transplanting them to outer space.

EXERCISE 4-C   *If possible, combine each of the following groups of two sentences into a single sentence each by making a half-sentence of one of the sentences and then attaching it to the other. Use any of the methods discussed in this chapter.*

LANGUAGE ACQUISITION BY APES

1. A number of experiments have been conducted in recent years.
   These experiments deal with teaching language to animals.

2. Most of the experiments use apes.
   The apes live in human-like conditions.

3. Often the apes have human "parents."
   Their human "parents" work with them constantly.

4. Linguists assume that some apes possess the intelligence for language but lack the necessary vocal equipment.
   Linguists have developed several different ways for the apes to "talk" without speaking.

5. One experiment used colored plastic shapes as substitutes for spoken words.
   One experiment succeeded in teaching a chimpanzee to communicate with her trainers.
   The chimpanzee was named Sarah.

6. Another experiment provided a chimpanzee with a special, color-coded computer keyboard.
   It learned to communicate with humans by punching the correct keys.

7. Another experiment used gorillas instead of chimpanzees.
   In another experiment people taught American Sign Language to these great apes.
   American Sign Language is normally used for communication between deaf people.

8. The language ability of these apes is not equal to that of humans.
   The language ability of these apes is still amazing.

5. Compound Half-Sentences

Two or more half-sentences may be compounded with *and, or, but,* or *yet* and attached to the same main sentence.

Simple	Combined
John was walking to school this morning. John noticed the cherry trees were blooming. John knew that spring had arrived.	1. *Walking to school this morning and noticing the cherry trees were blooming,* John knew that spring had arrived. 2. John, *walking to school this morning and noticing the cherry trees were blooming,* knew that spring had arrived.
Mary felt tired. Mary was determined to finish the job. Mary continued working.	1. *Feeling tired yet determined to finish the job,* Mary continued working. 2. Mary, *feeling tired yet determined to finish the job,* continued working.

6. Subordinators and Prepositions with Half-Sentences

6.1   **Time subordinators** such as *while, when, after, before,* etc. may be placed at the front of half-sentences beginning with *-ing* verb forms.

> **While** running down the street, George was attacked by a dog.
> **When** writing English, one should think about both form and meaning.
> **After** winning the game, the team was happy.

6.2   The **contrast subordinator** *although* can be used with *d-t-n* forms in some half-sentences.

> **Although** beaten by their rivals, the home team was not discouraged.

6.3   Certain **prepositions** such as *by, for, in, on,* and *upon* may also be placed at the front of half-sentences beginning with *-ing* verb forms.

> **By** working hard, Albert got a promotion.
> **For** settling the dispute, Henry received the Nobel Peace Prize.
> **In** studying for the test, students must use their textbooks.
> **On** (upon) entering the room, George smelled smoke.

EXERCISE 6-A   *Write at least twenty basic sentences of your own on the topic of* **pets**. *Combine these sentences using any of the methods that have been presented up to this point. Write your combined sentences in paragraph form.*

EXERCISE 6-B   *Write at least twenty basic sentences of your own on the topic of* **wild animals**. *Combine these sentences using any of the methods that have been presented up to this point. Write your combined sentences in paragraph form.*

EXERCISE 6-C   *Write at least twenty basic sentences of your own on the topic of* **farm animals**. *Combine these sentences using any of the methods that have been presented up to this point. Write your combined sentences in paragraph form.*

12

Clauses That Modify

This chapter will help you combine simple sentences and their parts correctly while avoiding or correcting mistakes like these:

- I am always the one that ___ doing the work.
- They were talking about the boys that <u>they</u> won the state tournament.
- Quarreling is a common thing ___ happens everywhere.
- The house I was in was exactly the place <u>which</u> the massacre happened.
- Jose teaches in the school of tourism which <u>is</u> a bachelor's degree.
- <u>Although</u> I studied hard, <u>but</u> I didn't pass the test.
- <u>When we ride on the bus, if we see an old lady.</u> We stand up and let her have a seat.
- One level of speaking is casual <u>that we usually use with our friends.</u>
- <u>Even</u> they know the penalty, they still break the rule.
- I'd like to write about a custom in my culture___has had a positive influence in my life.
- We left Guangzhou by train <u>which is a 45-minute ride to Kowloon.</u>

1. Subordinate Adverbial Clauses

1.1 Another method of combining two (or more) related sentences is to make a subordinate adverbial clause of one (or more) of them and attach it to the front or end of the main sentence as a shifter. To make a subordinate adverbial clause from a sentence, a word called a **subordinator** is placed in front of it.

Here are some common subordinators categorized by their general meaning:

time		cause or reason	condition	contrast or concession
after as as long as before next time now once	since the next time until (till) when whenever while	as as long as because now (that) since so (that) whereas	else if in case that unless whatever where whether	although even though though while whereas

The choice of a subordinator is determined by the relationship between the sentences to be combined.

When a subordinator is added to a sentence, this sentence becomes a **subordinate clause**. It is no longer a sentence and cannot be used alone. If it is used by itself, it is incorrect and called a **sentence fragment**.

1.2 Only one of the two methods—compounding (Chapter 9) or subordinating—can be used for combining two sentences.

John loved Grace. John married Susan.
correct → *Although* John loved Grace, he married Susan. (subordination)
correct → John loved Grace, *but* he married Susan. (compounding)
incorrect → *Although* John loved Grace, *but* he married Susan.

1.3 When subordinators are used, the sentences do not have equal weight as they do in compounds. Subordinate clause shifters have less weight than the main sentence. If one sentence is more important than the other(s), it should be the main sentence (except when the relationship between sentences is cause or reason). Make the less important sentence a shifter by putting a subordinator in front of it.

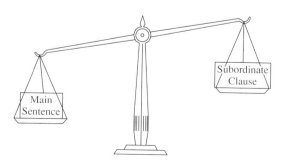

> John loved Grace. John married Susan.
>
> *Although John **loved** Grace,* he **married** Susan.
>   (The girl he married is given more importance.)
>
> *Although John **married** Susan,* he **loved** Grace.
>   (The girl he loved is given more importance.)

When the relationship between two sentences is cause or reason, the sentence which shows cause or reason becomes the subordinate clause.

> The dog looked fierce. (cause)
> The boy was afraid. (effect)
>
> *Because the dog looked fierce,* the boy was afraid.

1.4   Subordinate adverbial clauses may be used in either front or end shifter position. When they are used as front shifters, a comma is used to separate them from the main sentence. Normally, no comma is used when they follow the main sentence.

> The boy was afraid *because the dog looked fierce.* (no comma)
> *Because the dog looked fierce,* the boy was afraid.

1.5   Clauses beginning with the subordinator *if* often indicate conditions which are not really true. In these cases, special verb forms are employed to show the unreal conditions. This is explained in Chapter 6, section 11.

> *If I **have** the money,* I **will** buy a new car.   (real condition—I may have the money.)
> *If I **had** the money,* I **would** buy a new car.   (unreal condition—I don't have the money.)

EXERCISE 1-A   *Find the subordinate clauses in the following passage. Underline and label each one* time, cause, reason, condition, *or* contrast/concession, *depending on its relationship to the main sentence. The first one has been done for you.*

COOKBOOK RECIPES

[1]If you want to be a good cook, you will need a top quality cookbook.

condition

[2]Whatever culinary talent you might have, the ability to follow a recipe is of great importance. [3]Don't be embarrassed because you have to depend on cooking instructions. [4]Even the best cooks depend on the recipes of others when they are learning to prepare a new dish.

[5]After you become familiar with a recipe, you can experiment and modify it. [6]If your experiment succeeds, you can make a note and change the recipe for

use on future occasions. [7]If your experiment fails, be sure to note what made it fail. [8]You will not make the same mistake twice unless you forget to make a note of it.

EXERCISE 1-B   *Find the subordinate clauses in the following passage. Underline and label each one* time, cause, reason, condition, *or* contrast/concession, *depending on its relationship to the main sentence.*

SUPERSTITIONS

[1]Although many people say they don't believe in them, superstitions are very much a part of our lives. [2]Even though they won't admit it, many educated people still perform superstitious actions. [3]If they spill some salt, they are quick to throw a pinch of it over their left shoulder. [4]They may do this simply out of habit or because they really believe that it will keep bad luck and the devil away. [5]When they hear someone sneeze, many modern people say, "Bless you." ([6]This centuries-old practice developed because people believed that when a person sneezed his soul left his body.) [7]Unless they know they are being watched, many members of our "scientific" society will go out of their way to avoid walking under a ladder. [8]The next time you take a test, look around the room. [9]You may notice several classmates carrying good luck charms even though they will never admit that they *really* believe in them.

EXERCISE 1-C   *Find the subordinate clauses in the following passage. Underline and label each one* time, cause, reason, condition, *or* contrast/concession, *depending on its relationship to the main sentence.*

COMIC BOOKS

[1]Because they are cheap and because they are easy to read, comic books are very popular. [2]Even though comic books have little educational or literary value, people buy them because they are entertaining. [3]If a person cannot read well, he or she can still enjoy a comic book. [4]The pictures will tell a person what is happening when he or she can't understand the written words. [5]Young children are the greatest fans of comic books, since the simple yet action-packed plots of the stories that the books contain appeal to uneducated intellects. [6]The low prices of comic books also match the limited budgets of most school children. [7]Although they can't afford hardcover books, young people usually have enough money to buy inexpensive comic books. [8]Other children are even more careful with expenses and trade their old comic books with friends whenever they can.

[9]Some adult comic book fans keep "classic" issues and collect them until they have outstanding collections. [10]Although the comic books cost little originally, as "classics" they are worth a great deal.

EXERCISE 1.1-A   *Combine the sentences in each of the groups below by using subordinators. Make sure that you understand the relationship between sentences so that you can select an appropriate subordinator.*

TELEVISION PROGRAMS

1. Television programs change frequently in the United States.
   The tastes of TV viewers change constantly.

2. The major TV networks spend millions of dollars to find out what the viewing public wants to see.
   The competition between networks is keen.

3. A sensitive rating system is used to determine program popularity.
   Ratings change nearly every week.

4. A program is popular.
   TV stations charge a lot of money for a few seconds of advertising time.

5. A particular program increases in popularity.
   The price of advertising during that program goes up.

6. The cost of advertising is lower.
   Less popular programs are broadcast.

7. Program times are shuffled.
   TV stations want to broadcast the most popular programs at the best viewing times.

8. A program may be very educational or beneficial in some other way.
   Its popularity with the viewing public is the only thing that is evaluated.

EXERCISE 1.1-B   *Combine the sentences in each of the groups below by using subordinators. Make sure that you understand the relationship between sentences so that you can select an appropriate subordinator.*

EARTHQUAKES

1. Compression or tension stresses build up on the earth's surface.
   The earth moves and earthquakes occur.

2. There is a sudden release of stress.
   The movement causes vibrations to pass through and around the earth.

3. Wave vibrations travel through the land.
   Uplifts and landslides occur.

4. Buildings and chimneys fall.
People are killed or hurt.

5. The vibrations pass through the sea.
Tsunamis or tidal waves occur.

6. Tidal wave warning systems have been in operation.
Many people have escaped being washed out to sea.

7. No one knows when or where an earthquake will occur.
Scientists have ideas about where earth stresses are building up.

8. Earthquakes can be predicted.
Many lives will be saved.

EXERCISE 1.1-C   *Combine the sentences in each of the groups below by using subordinators. Make sure that you understand the relationship between sentences so that you can select an appropriate subordinator.*

ARABLE LAND

1. People cannot live everywhere on earth.
Seventy percent of the earth's surface is water.

2. People cannot cultivate all the land on the earth.
Thirty percent of the land area is covered with frozen ice or glaciers.

3. Very little rain falls on some parts of the land.
Deserts cover much of the land area.

4. Engineers have reclaimed some desert land.
Much desert land will never be reclaimed.

5. In some areas, once fertile land has become desert.
These areas are limited.

6. Floods and tides have eroded away much arable land.
Engineers have reclaimed some of the shallow ocean floors.

7. People have built reservoirs for water storage.
Desert land has been cultivated successfully.

8. People can utilize the sea.
Less land will be needed to raise food.

2. Relative Adjectival Clauses

2.1 When two sentences have a common noun, one sentence may be used to modify that noun in the other sentence. The modifying sentence is turned into a relative clause. This relative clause functions as an adjective and is placed after the noun it modifies. (See Chapter 8, section 2)

A **relative pronoun** is used in place of the subject or object of the sentence that is changed to a relative clause. The following function words are used as relative pronouns:

who	for the **subject** of the modifying sentence when that subject is **human**
whom	for the **object** of the modifying sentence when that object is **human**
which	for the **subject** or **object** of the modifying sentence when that object is **not human**
that	for the **subject** or **object** of the modifying sentence whether that subject/object is **human** or **not human**
where	for a **place**
when	for a **time**
whose	for a **possessive noun** or **possessive pronoun** whether it is **human** or **not human**

2.2 To combine two sentences in this way, follow the steps below:

Step 1. Start with two related sentences with a noun in common. (Any of the basic sentence patterns may be used.)

> The man robbed the bank.
> The man was wearing a ski mask.

Step 2. Decide which sentence will become the modifying clause. (This should be the least important of the two sentences.)

> The man was wearing a ski mask. (main sentence)
> The man robbed the bank. (modifying sentence)

Step 3.   Substitute the appropriate relative pronoun (*who, whom, which, that,* etc.) for the noun the two sentences have in common.

> The man was wearing a ski mask. (main sentence)
> *who* robbed the bank (relative clause)

Step 4.   Place the modifying clause after the noun it modifies.

> The man who robbed the bank was wearing a ski mask.

Here is another step-by-step example:

> ***Step 1.*** The man robbed the bank.
>   The bank is on Main Street.
>
> ***Step 2.*** The man robbed the bank. (main sentence)
>   The bank is on Main Street. (modifying sentence)
>
> ***Step 3.*** The man robbed the bank. (main sentence)
>   that is on Main Street (relative clause)
>
> ***Step 4.*** The man robbed the bank that is on Main Street.

2.3   Here are some additional examples illustrating more uncommon (and somewhat more sophisticated) relative clause combinations. Notice that in many of them the relative pronoun is embedded in a phrase.

> That is an idea.
> Its (the idea's) time has come.
>   That is an idea **whose** time has come.
>
> She is an executive.
> Her (the executive's) career is inspiring.
>   She is an executive **whose** career is inspiring.
>
> The terrorists robbed the passengers.
> Many of them (the passengers) were tourists on vacation.
>   The terrorists robbed the passengers, **many of whom** were tourists on vacation.
>
> I was attacked by several large men.
> One of them (the men) had an ugly scar on his cheek.
>   I was attacked by several large men, **one of whom** had an ugly scar on his cheek.
>
> Harry had a good eye for race horses.
> Several of them (the race horses) won big money for him.
>   Harry had a good eye for race horses, **several of which** won big money for him.

2.4   When the noun in common is the **object** of the modifying sentence, an additional step (3A) must be added.

Step 1.	The man wasn't wearing a ski mask.
	The police captured the man.
Step 2.	The man wasn't wearing a ski mask. (main sentence)
	The police captured the man. (modifying sentence)
Step 3.	The man wasn't wearing a ski mask. (main sentence)
	The police captured *whom* (*whom* is used because the noun it replaces is used as the object in this sentence)
Step 3A.	Move the relative pronoun (*whom*) to the front of the relative clause: *whom* the police captured
Step 4.	The man whom the police captured wasn't wearing a ski mask.

2.5   The relative pronoun *that* is sometimes used in place of any of the other relative pronouns (especially if the information in the relative clause is needed to identify the noun it modifies [see section 2.7 below]) except *whose*.

> The man *that* robbed the bank was wearing a ski mask.
> The man robbed the bank *that* was on Main Street.
> The man *that* the police captured wasn't wearing a ski mask.

2.6   If the relative pronoun replaces the **object** of the modifying sentence, it is possible to leave out the relative pronoun.

> The man the police captured wasn't wearing a ski mask.

The relative pronoun **cannot** be left out if it replaces the **subject** of the modifying sentence.

2.7   When the information provided by the relative clause is needed to identify the noun it modifies, no commas are used to set off the relative clause.

> The person who wrote that book certainly had some wild ideas.

Commas are used to set off a relative clause when the noun that the clause modifies has an identity independent of the information provided by the clause. (This is explained in greater detail in Chapter 14, section 2.)

> George Washington, who was the first President of the United States, is known as the father of his country.

The use or non-use of commas to set off a relative clause may change the meaning of the sentence.

The students who were late missed the exam. (Only the late students missed the exam.)

The students, who were late, missed the exam. (All the students referred to were late and all of them missed the exam.)

The politicians refused to vote for a tax increase, which would hurt the economy. (The relative clause is set off with a comma because it is not necessary to identify the type of tax increase. Interpretation: Any tax increase would hurt the economy. Don't worry about a tax increase.)

The politicians refused to vote for a tax increase that would hurt the economy. (The relative clause is not set off with a comma because it is necessary to identify the type of tax increase. Interpretation: Some tax increases hurt the economy; others don't. Watch out for higher taxes.)

EXERCISE 2-A *Find the relative and subordinate adverbial clauses in the passage below and underline them. Draw an arrow from each relative clause to the noun that it modifies.*

COLOR

[1]Color is a strange thing. [2]It exists in light which seems colorless to human eyes. [3]It does not exist in soap bubbles, rainbows, or paint, which all appear colored. [4]The colorful world that we see around us is not really many-hued. [5]Objects which seem colored appear a certain shade because their surfaces reflect back part of the light that is hitting them. [6]Thus, an apple looks red because it reflects red light. [7]The apple, which appears red, is not really that color.

[8]An object that appears to be one color one moment and another color a moment later–such as oil on water–does not really change color. [9]Colors play tricks like these because light sources and reflective surfaces vary.

EXERCISE 2-B *Find the relative and subordinate adverbial clauses in the passage below and underline them. Draw an arrow from each relative clause to the noun that it modifies.*

THE HORSESHOE CRAB

[1]The horseshoe crab, which is also called a king crab, has a body which is shaped like a horseshoe. [2]Scientists who study this creature, which is related to the spider, say it is not a true crab. [3]Its mouth, which has no jaws, is flanked by a pair of pincers that crush worms and other food. [4]It can burrow through sand or mud because of its five pairs of walking legs. [5]Horseshoe crabs, which are found along the Atlantic Coast, look for food along the bottom of the ocean. [6]Although the water is not clear, the crabs seem to see very well. [7]They can pick out things that other animals do not see. [8]Things that are black appear blacker and things that are white appear whiter to the crab. [9]This crab, which lives in shallow water, sometimes grows to be nearly two feet long.

EXERCISE 2-C   *Find the relative and subordinate adverbial clauses in the passage below and underline them. Draw an arrow from each relative clause to the noun that it modifies.*

BODY LANGUAGE

[1]People who speak different languages realize they have problems communicating. [2]However, gestures, which everyone frequently uses, are often considered to have only one meaning. [3]People who live in Europe and America think that a nod of the head, which is a gesture all people use, must mean a positive yes. [4]Although most people believe a nod means yes, this is not true in all cultures. [5]Some cultures use a nod to signify no. [6]The sign for OK, which is familiar to all people in the United States, is an obscene gesture in some countries that are located south of the border. [7]Anyone who expects to communicate with people who live in other cultures should try to understand both the verbal language, which can usually be learned through textbooks and teachers, and the meaningful gestures that accompany that language and are often overlooked by language learners.

EXERCISE 2.1-A   *Combine each of the following groups of sentences by making one (or more) of them a relative clause and using it to modify the noun that it has in common with the other(s).*

ENDANGERED SPECIES

1. The great dodo bird once lived in the Mascarene Islands in the Indian Ocean.
   The great dodo bird could not fly.

2. Dodo birds were bigger than turkeys.
   Until the 1600s there were many dodo birds.

3. Then, however, people went to the Mascarene Islands.
   People killed many dodo birds.

4. There were no laws to protect these dodo birds.
   These dodo birds soon became extinct.

5. More recently, the beautiful whooping crane began to die out.
   The beautiful whooping crane is found in America.

6. At one time there were only about fifty whooping cranes.
   The whooping cranes were rapidly disappearing.

7. People became concerned about whooping cranes.
   People enacted laws to protect them.

8. In the nineteenth century, hundreds of thousands of buffalo were killed indiscriminately.
    Hundreds of thousands of buffalo once lived in North America.

9. Hunters killed the buffalo for sport.
    Hunters almost annihilated the animals.

10. The buffalo almost died out.
    The buffalo once roamed the great plains.

11. The buffalo are now protected by law.
    The buffalo are no longer an endangered species.

12. One hopes that the whooping crane and the buffalo will never be as dead as the dodo.
    The whooping crane and the buffalo were once nearly extinct.

EXERCISE 2.1-B   *Combine each of the following groups of sentences by making one (or more) of them a relative clause and using it to modify the noun that it has in common with the other(s).*

FROM TYPEWRITER TO WORD PROCESSOR

1. The first typewriter was invented in 1714 by Henry Mill.
    The first typewriter was not very practical.
    Henry Mill lived in England.

2. A different typewriter was invented in 1829 by an American.
    A different typewriter was the first practical typewriter.
    The American called it a "typographer."

3. Nevertheless, these early typewriters were still not very practical.
    Most of these early typewriters typed only capital letters.
    Many of these early typewriters produced embossed writing.
    The embossed writing was intended for use by the blind.

4. The first electric typewriters did not appear until 1935.
    The first electric typewriters allowed typists to produce uniformly dark characters with greater speed and less effort.

5. In the early twentieth century, the stock ticker revolutionized the business world.
    The stock ticker was a kind of "automatic" typewriter.

6. Later, communications networks came to depend on the teletype.
   The teletype was another kind of automatic, electrical typewriter.

7. The teletype converted electrical impulses into typed news stories.
   The electrical impulses were sent by telephone or telegraph.

8. Nowadays, these machines have been replaced by computers.
   Computers can perform all their functions and many more.

9. In modern offices, word processors have taken the place of typewriters.
   Word processors allow on-screen corrections and rapid printing of documents.

10. With a modem, computers in distant locations can share data.
    A modem sends computer signals over telephone lines.

11. Someday, the traditional typewriter may be nothing but a historical relic.
    The traditional typewriter played an important role in our lives for over a century.

EXERCISE 2.1-C   *Combine each of the following groups of sentences by making one (or more) of them a relative clause and using it to modify the noun that it has in common with the other(s).*

INVENTIONS AND INVENTORS

1. Our modern lifestyle is the product of centuries of cumulative inventions.
   Our modern lifestyle depends on many technical devices.

2. Some of these devices, like the safety pin, are very common.
   The safety pin was invented in 1849 by Walter Hunt.

3. We take most of these common devices for granted.
   Many of these common devices are indispensable to the lives we live.

4. Do you ever think of Johann Gutenberg when you are reading a book?
   Johann Gutenberg invented printing with movable type around 1440.

5. Do you feel grateful to Thomas Edison when you want to read at night?
   Thomas Edison's inventions included the incandescent light bulb.

6. How would you listen to your portable radio if there were no batteries?
   Alessandro Volta invented batteries in the early 1800s.

7. Can you imagine how different your clothing would be without zippers? Zippers were invented by W. L. Judson in 1891.

8. In a way, Elisha G. Otis made skyscrapers and large, compact cities possible. Elisha G. Otis developed the modern elevator in 1853.

9. More important than zippers and elevators is the magnetic compass. The magnetic compass was invented in China about 1150 A.D. The magnetic compass encouraged worldwide exploration and discovery.

10. Perhaps the most important invention of all is paper. The most important invention of all made most of the others possible. Tsai Lun is credited with inventing paper in China about 50 A.D.

EXERCISE 2.2-A   *Write ten pairs of related sentences on the topic of* **trees** *or* **plants**. *In each pair, both sentences should have at least one noun in common. Then, whenever possible, combine each pair of sentences by making one of them into a relative clause that modifies the noun they have in common. Pay attention to meaning and use your best judgment. Some combinations may not be possible or advisable.*

EXERCISE 2.2-B   *Write ten pairs of related sentences on the topic of* **houses** *or* **buildings**. *In each pair, both sentences should have at least one noun in common. Then, whenever possible, combine each pair of sentences by making one of them into a relative clause that modifies the noun they have in common. Pay attention to meaning and use your best judgment. Some combinations may not be possible or advisable.*

EXERCISE 2.2-C   *Write ten pairs of related sentences on the topic of* **clubs**, **unions**, *or* **churches**. *In each pair, both sentences should have at least one noun in common. Then, whenever possible, combine each pair of sentences by making one of them into a relative clause that modifies the noun they have in common. Pay attention to meaning and use your best judgment. Some combinations may not be possible or advisable.*

3. Variety in Writing

A number of sentence transforming and combining methods have been presented in the last four chapters:

Compounds (Chapter 9)
Passive Transformation (Chapter 10)
Half-sentences (Chapter 11)
Subordinate adverbial clauses and Relative clauses (Chapter 12)

Good writing in English requires **variety** in

1. basic sentence patterns (Chapter 7),
2. types of sentence combinations (some compounds, some clauses, some half-sentences, etc.), and
3. sentence length (some short sentences and some long sentences).

Notice the variety of sentence combinations in the following passage:

THE SEMINOLE WARS

[1]On Christmas morning, 1837, the Seminoles and Miccosukees joined forces
<u>   </u>
                                        compound subject

for one last desperate attempt to turn back the United States troops. [2]In a fierce

battle which occurred near Lake Okeechobee, the Indians were driven off by
      <u>   </u>
                   relative clause

soldiers led by Zachary Taylor. [3]They left many casualties on the United States
        <u>   </u>
               half-sentence

side before they fled into the sanctuary of the Everglades.
    <u>   </u>
                subordinate adverbial clause

[4]This was the last major encounter of the Second Seminole War

although the bloody fighting continued sporadically. [5]On August 14, 1842 the
<u>   </u>
            subordinate adverbial clause

war ended. [6]Taking the lives of nearly 1,500 field troops and probably as many
            <u>   </u>
                                half-sentence

Indians, this war cost the United States about $20 million.
<u>   </u>

[7]In 1848, a band of some 360 Indians remaining in Florida were goaded into
                                        <u>   </u>
                                             half-sentence

an uprising that has been given the exaggerated title of the Third Seminole War.
          <u>   </u>
                           relative clause

[8]Aging Chief Billy Bowlegs was the leader of about 120 warriors

engaged in the rebellion. [9]After a series of minor skirmishes which occurred in
<u>   </u>   <u>   </u>
      half-sentence   relative clause
                            <u>   </u>
                                       subordinate adverbial clause

Central and South Florida, the Indians were subdued and repatriation to
<u>   </u>   <u>   </u>
    relative clause (cont.)   compound sentence
<u>   </u>
  subord. adv. clause (cont.)

the West went on as usual. [10]Ten years later the majority of
<u>   </u>
  compound sentence (cont.)

the Indians had been eliminated or removed. [11]Only a determined few
                      <u>   </u>
                          compound verb

who had fled deep into the Everglades remained in Florida. [12]By 1908 the
<u>   </u>
               relative clause

Seminoles living in Florida numbered about 275.
          <u>   </u>
              half-sentence

EXERCISE 3-A   *Combine the following sentences using a variety of methods. First, rearrange the sentences so that related sentences are near each other. Then combine them using the various methods presented in Chapters 8 through 12. Write your sentences in paragraph form.*

THE BASTILLE

The Bastille was in France.

The Bastille was one of the most famous prisons in the world.

The Bastille was originally a fortress.

The Bastille was located in the heart of Paris.

Later the Bastille was turned into a prison.

Those who offended the King of France were imprisoned in the Bastille.

Many political prisoners spent their whole lives in the Bastille.

No sunlight reached the cells in the Bastille.

No sunlight reached the prisoners.

The prisoners in the Bastille were liberated in the French Revolution.

The Bastille was stormed by the people of Paris.

The people stormed the Bastille during the French Revolution.

The people released the prisoners.

The people completely demolished the Bastille.

The Bastille was a hated symbol of oppression.

EXERCISE 3-B   *Combine the sentences below using a variety of methods. First, rearrange the sentences so that related sentences are near each other. Then combine them using the various methods presented in Chapters 8 through 12. Write your sentences in paragraph form.*

PERCEPTION

No two people see things exactly alike.

The exact same image may be reproduced upon the retina of the eye.

The brain recalls past experience.

The brain interprets that image.

An Eskimo is exposed to very few very colorful flowers.

A Polynesian is exposed to many very colorful flowers.

A flower seems very brilliant to an Eskimo.

A flower may appear very pale to a Polynesian.

Artists see the same thing.

Artists react differently.

Artists interpret what they see in their paintings.

An artist's aim is to create a visual image.

An artist projects his intrepretation in his pictures.

EXERCISE 3-C   *Combine the sentences below using a variety of methods. First, rearrange the sentences so that related sentences are near each other. Then combine them using the various methods presented in Chapters 8 through 12. Write your sentences in paragraph form.*

RIGHT-SIDE-UPNESS

Many things considered natural or normal are learned.

From birth, man feels his feet on the ground.

From birth, man feels the pull of gravity from below.

He reaches up with his hands to get things.

He reaches down with his hands to pick up things.

"Upness" seems part of his nature.

"Downness" seems part of his nature.

A series of experiments shows this is not so.

Some special eyeglasses were invented by scientists.

Some special eyeglasses turned everything upside down.

Scientists wanted to test "up-side-downness."

Volunteers wore these eyeglasses all the time.

Volunteers became completely disoriented.

They reached up to tie their shoelaces.

They stepped down to try to go up stairs.

They had no coordination.

At first, some had to crawl to get across a room.

After a while they got along comfortably with the glasses.

They were able to ride bicycles.

They were able to ski.

Up-side-downness eventually seemed right to them.

They lived normal lives.

After several weeks the glasses were taken off.

The volunteers were again completely disoriented.

The volunteers had to go through another period of adjustment.

Right-side-upness is learned in infancy.

Right-side-upness is reinforced through life.

EXERCISE 3.1-A   *Write at least twenty basic sentences on the topic of* **post offices** *or* **banks**. *Combine the related sentences using any of the combining methods that have been presented up to this point. Write your combined sentences in paragraph form.*

EXERCISE 3.1-B   *Write at least twenty basic sentences on the topic of* **libraries** *or* **museums**. *Combine the related sentences using any of the combining methods that have been presented up to this point. Write your combined sentences in paragraph form.*

EXERCISE 3.1-C   *Write at least twenty basic sentences on the topic of* **church buildings** *or* **government buildings**. *Combine the related sentences using any of the combining methods that have been presented up to this point. Write your combined sentences in paragraph form.*

13

Noun Clauses
and Phrases

This chapter will help you combine simple sentences correctly while avoiding or correcting mistakes like these:

- I don't understand why <u>is she</u> studying so hard.
- It is important <u>doing</u> that.
- __ Wives should obey their husbands is an old tradition in China.
- I didn't expect <u>studying</u> so hard in this class.
- She knows __ speak French.
- I want to know what classes <u>are you</u> taking.
- She asked my sister __ call an ambulance.
- He heard some strange sounds and went to check <u>that</u> what sounds they were.
- Tom promised that he would come after he <u>would finish</u> his work.
- I have many experiences with <u>quarrel</u>.
- It was impossible <u>that anyone who got my key</u>.
- I enjoy <u>to eat</u>, don't you?

1. Noun Clauses with Introducers

1.1   It is possible for a complete sentence to take the place of a noun. This is done by placing a function word called an **introducer** in front of the sentence. The addition of this function word changes the sentence into a noun clause (which is no longer a complete sentence and cannot stand alone).

Here are some common **introducers**. They are used to change sentences into noun clauses:

that	if
how	whether or not
why	whether ... (or not)
whichever	whatever

1.2   A noun clause may be used as a subject, an object, or a complement in another sentence. This process is called *embedding*. It is somewhat like placing one box (the noun clause) inside another box (the main sentence).

The subject noun clause is always **singular** even though it may contain compound or plural nouns.

Basic Sentences	Combined Sentences
He passed the test. (*Something*) surprised his teacher. (subject)	*That he passed the test* surprised his teacher. (subject)
He passed the test. I don't know (*something*). (object)	I don't know *how he passed the test*. (object)
He passed the test. The surprise is (*something*). (complement)	The surprise is *that he passed the test*. (complement)

1.3   Noun clauses may be used as subjects, objects, or complements in any basic sentence pattern (these are explained in Chapter 7).

Sentence pattern No. 1: S-V-O	*That he refuses to work* affects everyone. (subject)
Sentence pattern No. 2: S-V	*Whether George goes or stays* doesn't matter. (subject)
Sentence pattern No. 3: S-V_L-C	*That he passed the test* seems impossible. (subject) It seems *that I have failed the test*. (complement)
Sentence pattern No. 4: S-*be*-C	*Why I failed the test* is a mystery to me. (subject) The problem was *that I never studied*. (complement)

1.4   *That* is the most commonly used introducer. To indicate more specialized meanings, however, other introducers may also be used. It is important to use an introducer that indicates the appropriate meaning.

how indicates **manner**	(In some manner) he did it. I don't know *how he did it*.
why indicates **reason**	(For some reason) he did it. I don't know *why he did it*.
if, whether, and *whether or not* indicate **alternatives**	He did it (or he didn't). I don't know *if he did it* (or not). I don't know *whether he did it* (or not). I don't know *whether or not he did it*.
whatever and *whichever* indicate **choice** of many options	(One of several) flavor(s) appeals to you. You may order whichever flavor appeals to you. You may order whatever flavor appeals to you.

1.5   When the main clause expresses a demand or requirement, the noun clause uses the *base* form of the verb. The rules about verbs and time and subject-verb agreement do not apply as they normally would. (Traditionally, this special situation is called **subjunctive mood**.)

I demand that you *be* here at 9:00 A.M. sharp!
It is important that we *be* ready for emergencies.
It became necessary that he *look* for a new job.
They request that you and your partner *come* to the party.

EXERCISE 1-A   *Combine each of the following sets of sentences by making one into a noun clause with an introducer and then writing the clause as the subject, object, or complement of the other sentence in place of the (something). The first one has been done for you as an example.*

SELF-EDUCATION

1. It is not always necessary to have a formal education to become well-educated. (Something) is a recognized fact.

   That it is not always necessary to have a formal education to become well-educated is a recognized fact.

2. The person who reads a variety of books, magazines, and newspapers can become well-educated. (Something) is widely known also.

3. A person does or does not educate himself. (Something) depends on his motivation to improve.

4. People react to situations. (Something) can teach lessons about human behavior.

5. A person can learn from his or her mistakes if he or she wants to.
   (Something) is widely recognized.

6. We use the information available to us.
   (Something) determines how well we learn from our experiences.

7. We take advantage of our opportunities to learn.
   (Something) is all up to us.

EXERCISE 1-B   *Combine each of the following sets of sentences by making one into a noun clause with an introducer and then writing the clause as the subject, object, or complement of the other sentence in place of the (something).*

COMPETITION: MENTAL VS. PHYSICAL

1. People like to play in competition.
   (Something) depends on the type of the game.

2. Some people like active sports.
   (Something) is a mystery to me.

3. Anyone would like to get battered and bruised in a football game.
   (Something) seems incredible to me.

4. Pros do it for money.
   (Something) is understandable.

5. Anyone can enjoy getting physically tackled and thrown around.
   I don't see (something).

6. Anyone who plays football for fun deserves all the battering he gets.
   I feel (something).

7. People match wits in intellectual competition.
   On the other hand, I can understand (something).

8. I enjoy mental rather than physical activity.
   (Something) is readily apparent.

EXERCISE 1-C   *Combine each of the following sets of sentences by making one into a noun clause with an introducer and then writing the clause as the subject, object, or complement of the other sentence in place of the* (something).

POLYNESIAN NAVIGATORS

1. Few people realize (something).
   Some of the finest navigators in the history of the world were the early Polynesians.

2. Most modern Polynesians have forgotten (something).
   Their ancestors used the stars and ocean currents to sail across the wide Pacific Ocean without getting lost.

3. (Something) seems impossible.
   Ancient Polynesian navigators could sail from island to island across thousands of miles of ocean without technical instruments to guide them.

4. Many signs in the sky and the sea told the ancient Polynesians (something).
   They were on course or not.

5. Ancient Polynesian sailors knew (something).
   Certain cloud formations indicated the presence of an island.

6. Ocean current and swell patterns could tell them (something).
   They were going the right direction or sailing around in circles.

7. A pale green light reflected onto the underside of a cloud revealed (something).
   A low lying atoll whose shallow lagoon reflected the light was beneath the cloud.

8. The positions of numerous rising and setting stars on the horizon let the navigator know (something).
   He was sailing in the right direction.

9. Many modern Polynesians find it hard to explain (something).
   The art of navigating has been nearly completely lost among them.

10. (Something) is fortunate.
    The navigating art has been preserved by a few individuals.

2. Noun Clauses and Dummy Subjects

2.1 When a long noun clause introduced by *that* is used as the **subject** of a sentence, it is normally "postponed" (put after the predicate but before any end shifters). When this is done the **dummy subject** *it* (explained in Chapter 3, section 4) is placed in the normal subject position (after any front shifters). The dummy subject *it* is always **singular**.

> *That he loves her with all his heart* is obvious.
>   noun clause
>
> *It* is obvious *that he loves her with all his heart.*
>   noun clause

2.2 When a noun clause introduced by *that* is used as the object, complement, or "postponed subject" of a sentence, the introducer *that* may sometimes be left out. However, caution should be exercised, as omitting the *that* may result in confusion.

> It appears ***that*** *we have lost the ball game.*
>   noun clause (complement)
>
> It appears *we have lost the ball game.*
>   noun clause (complement)
>
> I didn't know ***that*** *he was your uncle.*
>   noun clause (object)
>
> I didn't know *he was your uncle.*
>   noun clause (object)

EXERCISE 2-A   *Rewrite each of the following sentences by using the dummy subject* it *and placing the noun clause later in the sentence.*

IDENTIFICATION TAGS

1. That so many unknown soldiers have died and been buried in nameless graves seems sad.

2. That the United States armed forces issue metal identification tags to every soldier as part of his or her equipment is standard procedure.

3. That soldiers call these identification discs "dog tags" is common knowledge.

4. That soldiers wear these tags at all times is mandatory.

5. That at one time a soldier had to furnish his or her own identification tag if he or she wanted one seems strange to us.

6. However, that soldiers—even in combat—were not required to wear identification tags during the Civil War is not widely known.

7. That before dangerous battles soldiers often pinned on pieces of paper with their names written on them so they could be identified if killed has been documented.

8. That every individual should have an identifiable number tatoo rather than a tag for positive identification has been suggested.

EXERCISE 2-B   *Rewrite each of the following sentences by using the dummy subject* it *and placing the noun clause later in the sentence.*

TWIN LANGUAGE

1. That children learn language by imitating their parents has long been thought.

2. That young children must have a model to pattern their own language after has been assumed.

3. That these ideas are true or false has been difficult to demonstrate.

4. However, a few years ago, that two young twins invented their own language amazed the world.

5. That they were the only ones who understood their unique language surprised everyone.

6. At first, that they were only babbling and not truly communicating was suspected.

7. Later, that the sounds they made to each other were a true language was demonstrated.

8. That their language was not related to any other human language on earth astounded investigating linguists and psychologists.

9. That in the absence of contact with adult language the two young girls had created their own language became apparent.

10. Although it was unbelievable, that they had truly done it without a model or adult help could not be denied.

EXERCISE 2-C   *Rewrite each of the following sentences by using the dummy subject* it *and placing the noun clause later in the sentence.*

THE DEAD SEA SCROLLS

1. That they were making one of the most important manuscript discoveries of modern times was not suspected by the Bedouins who entered a cave near the shore of the Dead Sea in 1947.

2. That what they would find in the cave would throw a blinding new light on scholars' interpretations of the Old and New Testaments didn't even occur to them.

3. That they were merely treasure hunters and didn't follow proper archaeological procedures is lamentable.

4. That trained archaeologists would have ever made the discovery is highly unlikely, however, because of the large number of unexplored caves in that area.

5. That some Bible scholars reacted to the scroll discovery with skepticism is understandable.

6. That the discovery was not a hoax soon became apparent.

7. At first, that the discovery would revolutionize scholarly thinking about Biblical history was not suspected.

8. As time went by, that the seven leather and two copper scrolls were of inestimable value was proven beyond doubt.

9. That there are no more archaeological surprises awaiting the world has not been proven.

10. That more such discoveries will be made in the future is very possible.

3. Noun Clauses with Substitutors

3.1   Another way to make a noun clause is to use a function word called a **substitutor**. The substitutor **takes the place** of the subject, the object, the complement, a demonstrative, or an adverb of the sentence that is used as the noun clause.

The following function words are used as **substitutors** in noun clauses:

who	(for human subjects)	*when*	(for time)
whoever	(for choice of human subjects)	*where*	(for place)
whom	(for human objects)	*wherever*	(for choice of places)
whomever	(for choice of human objects)	*whose*	(for possessive nouns)
what	(for things)	*which*	(for a specific thing or a demonstrative)
whatever	(for choice of things)	*whichever*	(for choice of things)
how	(for manner)	*why*	(for reason)

3.2 Although these substitutors look like the function words used to form *wh*-questions (Chapter 7, section 11), noun clauses are **not questions**. Therefore, **normal word order is used in noun clauses**.

(*Somebody*) comes first.   (*Somebody*) gets the job.
  subject   subject

Whoever comes first (noun clause)
substitutor

Whoever comes first gets the job. (sentence with noun clause)
    noun clause

(*Somebody's*) homework hasn't been done.   The teacher wants to know (*something*).
  possessive   object

Whose homework hasn't been done (noun clause)
substitutor

The teacher wants to know *whose homework hasn't been done.* (sentence with noun clause)
                             noun clause

3.3 When a substitutor takes the place of an **object, complement,** or **adverb**, it is moved to the **front** of the noun clause. Except for this change, **normal word order** is followed (aux-words are not moved).

The class will elect (*somebody*) president.   I wonder (*something*)
                object   object

The class will elect *whom* (noun clause)
                  substitutor

Whom the class will elect (noun clause with substitutor moved to front)
substitutor

I wonder *whom the class will elect president.* (**Not** *whom will* the class elect president)
           noun clause

Your major is (*something*).   The counselor wants to know (*something*).
                 complement   object

Your major is *what* (noun clause)
                 substitutor

What your major is (noun clause with substitutor moved to front)
substitutor

The counselor wants to know *what your major is.* (**Not** *what is your major*)
                                         noun clause

John went (*somewhere*).   I don't know (*something*).
               adverb of place   object

John went *where* (noun clause)
               substitutor

Where John went (noun clause with substitutor moved to front)
substitutor

I don't know *where John went.* (**Not** *where did John go*)
                     noun clause

3.4   Noun clauses can be used as subjects, complements, and objects, regardless of the type of substitutor they employ.

I don't know *who won the game.* (subject substitutor)
                 noun clause (object)

Whatever happens to George affects all of us. (subject substitutor)
          noun clause (subject)

Robert told me *which girl he admired most.* (demonstrative substitutor)
                  noun clause (object)

I can't see *how the magician makes the girl disappear.* (adverb of manner substitutor)
                    noun clause (object)

I want to know *when he took the test.* (adverb of time substitutor)
                   noun clause (object)

EXERCISE 3-A   *Rewrite one of each of the following pairs of sentences into a noun clause using a substitutor. Then combine it with the other sentence.*

A STRANGE ENCOUNTER

1. My friend told me (something).
   A strange man came to her house last week (in some way).

2. She didn't know (something).
   He was (somebody).

3. She had no idea (of something).
   He had come from (somewhere).

4. She asked him (something).
   He needed (something).

5. She couldn't understand (something).
   He had come to her house (for some reason).

6. But she never found out (something) because he turned and walked away without saying a word.
   He wanted (something).

7. She didn't have any idea (of something).
   He went (somewhere).

8. He didn't tell her (something).
   He was going (somewhere).

9. He didn't even say (something).
   His name was (something).

10. She can still remember (something).
   He looked like (something).

11. She will never forget (something).
   He looked (in some way) desperate.

EXERCISE 3-B   *Rewrite one of each of the following pairs of sentences into a noun clause using a substitutor. Then combine it with the other sentence.*

STRANGE RECORDS

1. Recently I read (something).
   (In some way) people have established strange records.

2. I have often wondered (something).
   (Something) prompts people to do strange things.

3. (Something) surprised me.
   I read (something).

4. (Somebody) played a violin solo underwater.
   (Somebody) probably couldn't decide whether to bathe or play music.

5. I wonder (something).
   (Something) made a man walk clear across the country from New York to San Francisco playing a violin all the way.

6. I pondered on (something).
   (Something) happened to the man who ate sixty-three bananas in ten minutes.

7. I ruminated about (something).
   (Someone's) record was broken when a man downed fourteen eggs in one minute.

8. (Somebody) walked on his hands for 871 miles from Vienna to Paris.
   (Somebody) might have had foot troubles before this stunt.

9. But afterwards, I wonder (something).
   (Something) happened to his hands.

10. I have given up speculating on (something).
    (Something) may yet occur.

11. Still, a new edition of the world records book may tell me (something).
    Someone will have done (something) next.

EXERCISE 3-C   *Rewrite one of each of the following pairs of sentences into a noun clause using a substitutor. Then combine it with the other sentence.*

A CONFESSION

1. Nobody has any doubt about (something).
   It happened (somewhere).

2. Almost everybody knows (something).
   It happened (sometime).

3. Some have asked me (something).
   I did it (for some reason).

4. Others, more curious, ask me (something).
   I did it (in some way).

5. A few want to know (something).
   (Somebody) helped me.

6. I haven't told them (something).
   They want to know (something).

7. They don't know (something).
   I haven't told them (for some reason).

8. I really don't know (something).
   It happened (for some reason).

9. Nor do I know (something).
   It happened (in some way).

10. All I really know is (something).
   (Something) happened.

4. Noun Clauses and Reported Speech

4.1 Dialog representing actual speech between people can be reported in noun clauses. In such cases the main clause uses a **reporting word** like *said*. Other commonly used reporting words include the following:

added	*exclaimed*	*remarked*
admitted	*explained*	*repeated*
agreed	*maintained*	*replied*
announced	*noted*	*responded*
answered	*pleaded*	*stated*
asked	*pointed out*	*suggested*
commented	*proposed*	*testified*
confessed	*questioned*	*thought*
continued	*read*	*vowed*
declared	*related*	*warned*

4.2 The speech sentence is changed into a noun clause by using an **introducer** or **substitutor** such as *that, how, why,* or *if*. Introductory words like "Yes," "No," or "Of course" are usually removed. The noun clause is then inserted into the main (reporting) clause. **No quotation marks** are used.

Reporting clause	→	Howard said (something).
Actual speech	→	Howard: "The weather was cold."
Reported speech	→	Howard said *that* the weather was cold.
		<u> </u>
		noun clause

4.3   Since reported speech is about what someone said, it is necessary to **change any first person pronouns** (*I, me, my, mine; we, us, our, ours*) **to third person** (*he/she, him/her, his/her, his/hers; they, them, their, theirs*).

> Peter: "**I** was amazed at the way they treated **me**."
> Peter reported that **he** was amazed at the way they treated **him**.
>
> Mr. Smith: "**We** had a great time on **our** vacation."
> Mr. Smith commented that **they** had a great time on **their** vacation.

4.4   Since noun clauses are not questions, **question word order and hidden aux-words which are used to form questions are not used in reported speech** even though the original speech sentence may have been a question. Nevertheless, the introducer/substitutor and the *wh*-question word may have the same form.

> Rosemary: "**How was** the movie?"
> Rosemary asked **how** the movie **was**.
>
> The detective: "**Where did** the thief **go**?"
> The detective asked **where** the thief **went**.

4.5   Typically, the reporting is done in past tense even though present tense was used in the original speech sentence. In such cases, it is usually necessary to **change the present tense verbs and aux-words in the original speech sentence to their corresponding past tense forms** when creating the reported speech noun clause.

> Sharon: "I **have** been swimming."
> Sharon said that she **had** been swimming.
>
> Steven: "I **live** in that house."
> Steven told me that he **lived** in that house.

Nevertheless, in cases where the reported speech noun clause expresses a **general truth** or where the speaker wants to emphasize that the reported action is **still occurring**, present tense may be used.

> Eric: "Carol **lives** in Chicago now."
> Eric told me that Carol **lives** in Chicago now.
>
> Einstein: "*E* equals *MC* squared."
> Einstein maintained that *E* **equals** *MC* squared.

EXERCISE 4-A *Change the actual speech (in quotation marks) in the dialog below into reported speech using noun clauses.*

RETURNING HOME

1. Mary: "George is coming home soon."
   Mary remarked _____.

2. Martha: "Where is he?"
   Martha asked _____.

3. Mary: "He's stationed in Alaska, but his time is just about up."
   Mary replied _____.

4. Martha: "How long has he been in the army?"
   Martha asked _____.

5. Mary: "He first enlisted five years ago."
   Mary answered _____.

6. Martha: "It will be great to have him back!"
   Martha exclaimed _____.

7. Mary: "Oh yes, I couldn't agree more wholeheartedly!"
   Mary responded _____.

EXERCISE 4-B *Change the actual speech (in quotation marks) in the dialog below into reported speech using noun clauses.*

AN INVITATION TO THE CIRCUS

1. Tom: "Have you ever been to the circus?"
   Tom asked Jan _____.

2. Jan: "Of course I have."
   Jan responded _____.

3. Tom: "What part do you like best?"
   Tom questioned _____.

4. Jan: "I like the wild animals."
   Jan answered _____.

5. Tom: "My favorite part is the acrobats."
   Tom volunteered _____.

6. Jan: "Actually, I like everything about a circus."
   Jan bubbled _____.

7. Tom: "Do you know that there is one in town this week?"
   Tom then asked Jan _____.

8. Jan: "No, I didn't."
   She answered _____.

9. Tom: "Would you like to go to it?"
   Tom asked ———————————————————————.

10. Jan: "Sure! Nothing could keep me away!"
    Jan responded ———————————————————.

EXERCISE 4-C   *Change the actual speech (in quotation marks) in the dialog below into reported speech using noun clauses.*

LOST IN THE COUNTRY

1. Man: "Do you know the way to the airport?"
   The man asked the little boy ————————————————.

2. Boy: "No, I don't think so."
   The boy replied ——————————————————.

3. Man: "Do you ever see airplanes flying?"
   The man then asked ————————————————.

4. Boy: "Yes, I see them all the time."
   The boy answered ————————————————.

5. Man: "Where do they come from?"
   The man asked ——————————————————.

6. Boy: "They come from the other side of the lake."
   The boy responded ———————————————.

7. Man: "Where do they go?"
   The man inquired ————————————————.

8. Boy: "They go over the mountains."
   The boy said ——————————————————.

9. Man: "I must really be lost!"
   The man concluded ————————————————.

5. Noun Phrases from Predicates (Gerunds and Infinitives)

5.1   It is possible to use part of the predicate of a sentence as a noun phrase. Only predicates with **-*ing* verb forms** or with **base verb forms** can be used this way.

1. **-*ing* verb forms** (traditionally called **gerunds**). The aux-word must be removed when the predicate is used as a noun phrase.

Someone (subject)	/ was (aux-word)	passing the test. (predicate with *-ing* verb form)
	was /	*passing the test* noun phrase

2. **base verb forms**. The aux-word must be removed and the function word *to* is placed before the base form. (This combination is often called the **infinitive form**.)

Someone (subject)	/ will (aux-word)	pass the test. (predicate with base form)
	will /	*pass the test* *to pass the test* noun phrase

These noun phrases can be used as subjects, objects, and complements—with some restrictions.

Noun phrase as the subject of a sentence
Passing the test worried John.
To pass the test was his goal.

Noun phrase as the object of a verb
John tried *passing the test*.
John tried *to pass the test*.

Noun phrase as the object of a preposition
John worried about *passing the test*.
(*To* + base form cannot be used as the object of a preposition.)

Noun phrase as the complement of a sentence
John's goal is *passing the test*.
John's goal is *to pass the test*.

He seemed *to worry a lot*.
(Most linking verbs cannot be followed by an *-ing* noun phrase.)

5.2 Both *-ing* (gerund) and *to* + base (infinitive) noun phrases may be used as **objects** of some verbs. However, **both types cannot be used with all verbs**. Some verbs require the *-ing* form while others require the *to* + base form. (Appendix A, page 141, lists many of these verbs.)

Correct	→ He finished *doing* the job.
Incorrect	→ He finished *to do* the job.
Correct	→ He hoped *to do* the job.
Incorrect	→ He hoped *doing* the job.

5.3 *-ing* (gerund) and *to* + base (infinitive) noun phrases can also be used after the objects of certain verbs.

Subject	Verb	Object	Noun Phrase
He	asked	me	to help.
We	saw	him	coming.

Be careful! The forms are not freely interchangeable. As explained in section 5.2 above, the correct form to use (either *-ing* or *to* + base) depends on the verb in the main sentence.

Correct	→ They wanted us *to sing*.
Incorrect	→ They wanted us *singing*.
Correct	→ They heard us *singing*.
Incorrect	→ They hear us *to sing*.

5.4   The -*ing* noun phrase can be modified by **adjectives** and **possessives**.

> **Brilliant** *thinking* helped him on the test.
> (adjective)
>
> **His** *passing the test* delighted John.
> (possessive)

5.5   *to* + base (infinitive) noun phrases can be preceded by the following introducers or substitutors:

how	I can't figure out **how** *to do this.*
whether (or not)	We don't know **whether or not** *to trust him.*
who/whom	I don't know **whom** *to call.*
when	Please tell him **when** *to get off the bus.*
where	Please tell me **where** *to turn.*
which	I can't decide **which** *to buy.*
what	I don't know **what** *to buy.*

EXERCISE 5-A   *Write appropriate* noun phrases using -ing or to + base verb forms *in the blanks in the sentences below. Remember to maintain the continuity of thought in the paragraph.*

LEISURE TIME ACTIVITIES

1. I enjoy _____.

2. However, I don't like _____.

3. In the summer, _____ is fun.

4. But in the winter, it is impossible _____.

5. If I'm alone, I try _____.

6. When my friends are with me, we sometimes want _____.

7. At some time or another most of us have attempted _____.

8. We once agreed _____.

9. I have postponed _____.

10. However, at least once in my life, I hope _____.

EXERCISE 5-B   *Write appropriate* noun phrases using -ing or to + base verb forms *in the blanks in the sentences below. Remember to maintain the continuity of thought in the paragraph.*

MY VOCATION

1. When I was young, my mother wanted me _____.

2. She hoped _____.

3. But I didn't plan on _____.

4. I considered _____.

5. However, I reconsidered and decided _____.

6. I agreed _____,

7. and I intended _____.

8. I practiced _____.

9. I forgot _____,

10. although I meant _____.

11. Now I want _____.

12. I intend _____.

13. I plan on _____.

14. I expect _____.

EXERCISE 5-C   *Write appropriate* noun phrases using -ing or to + base verb forms *in the blanks in the sentences below. Remember to maintain the continuity of thought in the paragraph.*

A NEW SKILL

1. Last week I began _____.

2. _____ wasn't easy.

3. I couldn't help _____.

4. But I kept on _____.

5. Finally, I started _____.

6. I hoped _____.

7. I didn't expect _____.

8. However, I learned _____.

9. After a while, I stopped _____.

10. Then I missed _____.

11. Today, I will continue _____.

12. I plan on _____.

6. Noun Phrases and Dummy Subjects

The **dummy subject** *it* may also be used with noun phrases. However, only the *to* + base (infinitive) form can be used with the dummy subject *it*. If *-ing* phrases (gerunds) are used as the original subject, they must be changed to the *to* + base (infinitive) form when the dummy subject *it* is used.

> *Enduring hardship and cold* is the lot of an arctic explorer.
>   noun phrase
>
> It is the lot of an arctic explorer *to endure hardship and cold.*
>   noun phrase

EXERCISE 6-A　　*Rewrite each of the following sentences by using the dummy subject* it *and placing the noun clause or phrase later in the sentence.*

CITY VS. COUNTRY LIFE

1. That people like to live in a city is understandable.

2. On the other hand, that people like to live in the country is understandable also.

3. Seeing shows, attending concerts, participating in educational or political events, and eating in many different kinds of restaurants is a part of city life.

4. Enduring air pollution, noise, and crowds is also a part of city life.

5. That the country provides fresh air, a quiet peaceful atmosphere, and freedom from noxious traffic fumes cannot be denied.

6. Relaxing, jogging, hiking, and just plain loafing are great.

7. That some people find life in the country monotonous is true, however.

8. That others find life in the city disturbing and unsettling is equally true.

9. Living in the city but spending weekends and vacations in the country is a common (but expensive) solution.

EXERCISE 6-B　　*Rewrite each of the following sentences by using the dummy subject* it *and placing the noun clause or noun phrase later in the sentence.*

MUSIC

1. That "music hath charms to calm the savage beast" is an old adage.

2. That listening to music can affect human and animal emotional states has been demonstrated.

3. Tapping one's feet and swaying rhythmically is natural when listening to music with a strong beat.

4. That soft dreamy music has a soothing effect and may often cause people to doze or sleep has been observed.

5. That some music, like much that occurs at rock concerts, can induce hypnotic states of frenzy, particularly in emotionally immature people, seems probable.

6. That playing martial music at political or recruitment rallies promotes feelings of patriotism is well known.

7. Playing mysterious and eerie music on the sound track of spine-chilling movies is a common practice, thus creating a mood for what follows.

8. Watching a wild western without the accompanying music would not be nearly as exciting.

9. Even during the silent era of early movies, playing appropriate piano or organ music was necessary to set the mood and create the proper atmosphere for the screenplay.

10. That a silent world would be a monotonous world cannot be denied.

EXERCISE 6-C   *Rewrite each of the following sentences by using the dummy subject* it *and placing the noun clause or phrase later in the sentence.*

NUTRITION

1. That people need a balanced diet is a well known fact.

2. If people want to be healthy, eating foods from four basic food groups is necessary.

3. However, discovering this fact was not a simple task.

4. Once it was discovered, convincing people that it was true was an even greater job.

5. Changing people's eating habits was a great challenge.

6. Convincing English sailors that vitamin C from citrus fruit was necessary took much suffering and death from scurvy.

7. That people began to realize the value of vitamin D in their diet was not until after many thousands had been crippled by rickets.

8. Even today, getting people to change their dietary habits is not easy.

9. That adults cling to the customs they learned as children is obvious.

10. For example, even though brown rice is more nutritious than white rice, convincing people who think of it as animal feed that eating it would improve their health is extremely difficult.

7. Compound Noun Clauses Connected with Subordinators

7.1 Two or more noun clauses may be compounded in a single sentence by using a time subordinator (*while, when, after, before,* etc.). In some cases, other, non-time subordinators may be used also (e.g., *so . . . that*).

7.2 When this combination is done, the time of the **second** clause is shown by the subordinator, which relates it to the time indicated by the verb in the first clause. For this reason, in contrast to the normal usage of verb tenses to show time (explained in Chapter 6), the verb form in the second noun clause indicates **only simple present or past time** (or present or past in-progress if the subordinator is *while*), whichever is the established time.

Established past	Later time in the past
Alex **said** that . . .	he **would study**. (while) his roommates **would be** out.
Combined Alex said that he **would study** while his roommates **were** out.	

Established present	Later time in the present
The president **has assured** the people that . . .	he **will lower** taxes. (after) inflation **will be** controlled.
Combined The president has assured the people that he **will lower** taxes after inflation **is** controlled.	

EXERCISE 7-A   *Combine the pairs of noun clauses in each sentence below using the time subordinator indicated. Be sure to change the verb form in the second clause.*

TERRY'S AMBITION

1. Terry thought (that)   { she would like to train animals   (when)   she would grow up.

2. Terry expected (that)   { the animals would obey   (when)   she would give them a command.

3. She dreamed (that)   { the crowds at the circus would applaud loudly   (when)   the animals would obey her every command.

4. Terry didn't know (that)   { training animals would require years of work   (before)   they would obey.

5. She finally realized (that)   { animal training would take lots of effort   (before)   she would receive any fame.

6. She changed her mind and decided (that)   { she would be a business executive   (when)   she would become an adult.

EXERCISE 7-B   *Combine the pairs of noun clauses in each sentence below using the time subordinator indicated. Be sure to change the verb form in the second clause.*

SISTER KNOWS BEST

1. My younger brother, Harry, said (that)   { we had gone to Yellowstone Park   (when)   he had been five years old.

2. My older sister, Grace, insisted (that)   { we had gone to the Grand Canyon   (when)   he had been five.

3. Moreover, she distinctly remembered (that)   { we had visited Yellowstone   (before)   Harry had been born.

4. Her recollection was (that) {
we had vacationed in Yellowstone
(when)
I had been two years old.
}

5. Now, it is true (that) {
Harry had not been born
(until)
I had been three.
}

6. Nevertheless, Harry remembered (that) {
he had seen a live bear
(when)
he had been a small child.
}

As usual, Grace had a ready explanation.

7. She concluded (that) {
Harry had seen a live bear
(when)
he had visited the zoo.
}

8. He finally admitted (that) {
he had been so young
(that)
he hadn't known the difference between the zoo
and Yellowstone National Park.
}

EXERCISE 7-C   *Combine the pairs of noun clauses in each sentence below using the time subordinator indicated. Be sure to change the verb form in the second clause.*

A FAMILY GARDEN

1. Last winter my family decided (that) {
we would plant a garden
(when)
spring would come.
}

2. We dreamed (that) {
we would enjoy beautiful flowers and fresh vegetables
(when)
summer would arrive.
}

3. We planned (that) {
we would order seeds
(before)
the snow would melt.
}

4. Father decided (that) {
he and mother would prepare the ground
(while)
my brother and I would spread the fertilizer.
}

5. My brother and I agreed (that)
{
I would water the garden
(while)
he would pull the weeds.

6. Now that spring is here, we are beginning to see (that)
{
the garden will not grow
(while)
we will relax in the shade.

7. We realize (that)
{
we will have to give up many summer pleasures
(while)
the garden will be growing.

8. We have come to the conclusion (that)
{
we will have to invest our time and effort
(before)
we will be able to smell the flowers and eat the vegetables.

EXERCISE 7.1-A   *Write at least twenty basic sentences on the topic of* **exercise**. *Combine these sentences into a short essay using any of the combining methods that have been presented so far.*

EXERCISE 7.1-B   *Write at least twenty basic sentences on the topic of* **work**. *Combine these sentences into a short essay using any of the combining methods that have been presented so far.*

EXERCISE 7.1-C   *Write at least twenty basic sentences on the topic of* **education**. *Combine these sentences into a short essay using any of the combining methods that have been presented so far.*

14

Adding Information

This chapter will help you combine simple sentences correctly while avoiding or correcting mistakes like these:

- I love Mexican food, tacos, enchiladas, and burritos.
- Some students, including me don't trust that test.
- We enjoyed visiting Shanghai a city of twelve-million people.
- Our group also went to Japan a major competitor with the United States.
- George Washington who later became the first president of the United States was a brilliant and determined general.
- Teachers like students, who come to class prepared.
- Dogs and cats, running loose, are a menace to society.

1. Adding Nonessential Information

1.1   When one sentence contains information about a noun in another sentence, the two sentences may be combined. This information may be in the form of...

1. a **noun** or **noun phrase** (Chapter 13, section 5)
2. a **noun clause** (Chapter 13, sections 1 and 3)
3. a **relative clause** (Chapter 12, section 2)
4. a **half-sentence** (Chapter 11)

In these cases, the extra information is added immediately after the noun.
   Be careful! Both the subject of the extra information sentence and the noun which the extra information follows must be the same person or thing.

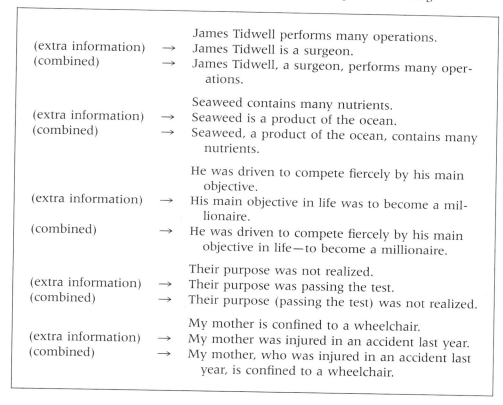

(extra information)	→	James Tidwell performs many operations.
	→	James Tidwell is a surgeon.
(combined)	→	James Tidwell, a surgeon, performs many operations.
(extra information)	→	Seaweed contains many nutrients.
	→	Seaweed is a product of the ocean.
(combined)	→	Seaweed, a product of the ocean, contains many nutrients.
(extra information)	→	He was driven to compete fiercely by his main objective.
	→	His main objective in life was to become a millionaire.
(combined)	→	He was driven to compete fiercely by his main objective in life—to become a millionaire.
(extra information)	→	Their purpose was not realized.
	→	Their purpose was passing the test.
(combined)	→	Their purpose (passing the test) was not realized.
(extra information)	→	My mother is confined to a wheelchair.
	→	My mother was injured in an accident last year.
(combined)	→	My mother, who was injured in an accident last year, is confined to a wheelchair.

1.2   Notice in all the examples above that the identity of the noun that the extra information follows is **clear without this added information**. Therefore, this extra information is **set off by punctuation marks**. Extra information added to a sentence may be set off in three different ways:

1. **Commas** are used when the information is closely related to the rest of the sentence.

> American Indians, the original inhabitants of the American continent, are very different from the people of India.
>
> The electric light bulb, invented by Thomas Edison, was first commercially produced in 1879.

2. **Dashes** are used when the extra information is not as closely related. They can also be used to avoid confusion when the extra information is closely related to the sentence but contains several items in a series separated by commas.

> American Indians—often called Amerindians—are very different from the people of India.
>
> The electric light bulb—an essential part of today's world—was first commercially produced in 1879.

3. **Parentheses** are used when the extra information is distantly related. Information which would not normally be a part of a sentence because of its distant relationship can be inserted between parentheses.

> American Indians (whom Columbus mistakenly thought were natives of South Asia) are very different from the people of India.
>
> The electric light bulb (how could we live without it today?) was first commercially produced in 1879.

EXERCISE 1-A

Rewrite the following sentences by combining them. Add the extra information from one sentence after the noun in the other sentence which is the same as the subject of the extra information sentence. Use commas, dashes, or parentheses as appropriate.

AUSTRALIAN ANIMALS

1. Some of the earth's most unusual animals are found in Australia.
   Australia is a continent widely separated from the rest of the world.

2. Most people know that Australia is the home of the kangaroo.
   The kangaroo is a large animal that carries its young in a pouch.

3. They don't often know that baby kangaroos weigh less than an ounce when born.
   Baby kangaroos may grow to weigh over a hundred pounds as adults.

4. For many weeks, the baby kangaroo never leaves the security of its mother's pouch.
   The baby kangaroo is born blind and helpless.

5. The model for the "teddy bear" was the Australian koala bear.
   The koala bear is not really a bear at all.

6. Koala bears are extremely shy and gentle.
   Koala bears eat the leaves of the eucalyptus tree.

7. The platypus may be the strangest of them all.
   The platypus has webbed feet and a duck bill.

8. The platypus also has a tail like a beaver's.
   The platypus lives near water and is an excellent swimmer.

9. Surprisingly, the platypus lays eggs.
   The platypus is covered with thick fur.

10. Other unusual animals are also found in Australia.
    Other unusual animals are the spiny anteater, the wallaby, the wombat, and the flying opossum.

EXERCISE 1-B   *Rewrite the following sentences by combining them. Add the extra information from one sentence after the noun in the other sentence which is the same as the subject of the extra information sentence. Use commas, dashes, or parentheses as appropriate.*

ILLEGAL ALIENS

1. Some people live in one country and work in another.
   One country is their homeland.

2. This is done legally or illegally.
   Legally is with proper papers.

3. In the United States, illegal aliens are periodically sent back to their own countries.
   Illegal aliens are people who have no legal right to be in the country.

4. A "guesstimate" places the number of illegal aliens in the United States at between three million and five million.
   A "guesstimate" is an unofficial, undocumented estimate.

5. Borders are often long and hard to patrol.
   Borders are boundaries between countries.

6. Border communities provide excellent cover for the people who manage to cross the border illegally.
   Border communities often have many thousands of legal immigrants.

7. Some illegal aliens return again and again to work in the United States.
   Illegal aliens are frequently agricultural workers from Mexico and other countries.

8. Charles Pérez contends that half of that city's downtown crime is related in some way to illegal immigration.
   Charles Pérez is a director for the Immigration and Naturalization Service in El Paso, Texas.

9. Employers of illegal immigrants violate regulations designed to protect the interests of U.S. workers and the immigrants.
   Employers of illegal immigrants are accused of abetting the problem.

10. As long as menial jobs in the United States pay many times what an immigrant can earn at home, illegal immigration will remain a problem.
    Menial jobs are those which require little or no skills.

EXERCISE 1-C   *Rewrite the following sentences by combining them. Add the extra information from one sentence after the noun in the other sentence which is the same as the subject of the extra information sentence. Use commas, dashes, or parentheses as appropriate.*

REFUGEES

1. One big problem in the world today is displaced persons.
   Displaced persons are expatriates without a homeland.

2. Among these are refugees.
   Refugees have problems locating in a new land.

3. Refugees are people without a country.
   Refugees are sometimes refused entry into countries to which they have fled.

4. Unlike the illegal alien, the refugee must seek asylum in another place.
   The illegal alien can return to his native land.

5. During rebellions, the losing leaders usually flee the country to avoid being jailed or put to death.
   Rebellions are internal strife within a country.

6. They must find refuge in another country.
   Another country is a neutral place.

7. During World War II, thousands of refugees were eventually relocated in Canada, the United States, and Australia.
   Thousands of refugees were Germans, Poles, Czechs, and other Europeans.

8. Before being legally accepted into the new countries, these refugees lived in displacement camps.
   Displacement camps are temporary barracks or shelters often surrounded by barbed wire.

9. & 10. Constant political upheaval has created a new world problem.
Constant political upheaval is the overturning of governments.
A new world problem is thousands and thousands of refugees.

2. Adding Essential Information

2.1 Sometimes nouns, noun phrases, or noun clauses added after a noun provide information that is **necessary to the identity of the noun** they follow. When the added information is essential to the identity of the noun that it follows, it is **not set off** with commas, dashes, or parentheses. (This idea was introduced in Chapter 12, section 2.7.)

> Elizabeth *the First* felt that Mary *Queen of Scots* was a threat and had her executed.
> The picture *hanging above the fireplace* is an original oil painting.
> All the students *who fail this class* must take it again.

2.2 A good test to determine if the information is or is not vital (whether commas, dashes, or parentheses should be used) is to take it out. If the **identity of the noun remains clear**, then the added information is **not necessary** and should be set off. If the noun is **not clearly identified** when the information is removed, commas, dashes, or parentheses should not be used since the information is **necessary**.

In the examples below, whether or not commas, dashes, or parentheses are used depends on the situation.

> My brother, Tom, will be here tonight. (I have only one brother. His name is Tom.)
> My brother Tom will be here tonight. (I have more than one brother.)
>
> The girl, standing near the window, is my cousin. (There is only one girl in the room.)
> The girl standing near the window is my cousin. (There is more than one girl in the room but only one near the window.)
>
> The students (who came late) missed the quiz. (All of the students we are talking about came late.)
> The students who came late missed the quiz. (Some of the students came late.)

EXERCISE 2-A   *Insert commas, dashes, or parentheses where necessary in the passage below.*

LANGUAGE

[1]My native language English is the most sensible language of all. [2]The grammar is logical and the vocabulary sensible. [3]This is not true of other languages such as Farsi or Finnish. [4]They seem to me a monolingual speaker of English to be illogical and senseless. [5]All students who study English do not feel the way

I do. [6]Some students who are always translating from their own languages feel that English cannot possibly be learned. [7]These students who speak their native languages at all times seem to find no logical order in English grammar. [8]The students who try to speak and write exclusively in English seem to do much better. [9]They have finally realized that any language Japanese, French, or Samoan has its own language structure which must be used as one speaks or writes the words of that tongue. [10]A language whatever it is is sensible and logical to the native speaker who has learned that language as part of the maturation process. [11]Somehow one internalizes sound differences and grammatical rules as he or she acquires the vocabulary of his or her native language.

EXERCISE 2-B   *Insert commas, dashes, or parentheses where necessary in the passage below.*

"PEANUTS"

[1]"Peanuts" a famous American cartoon strip was created by Charles Schulz over twenty-five years ago. [2]Schulz called Sparky by his friends has created many characters for his internationally known cartoon strip.

[3]Charlie Brown one of the original "Peanuts" characters is a boy who never wins. [4]Charlie Brown's dog Snoopy is perhaps the most widely known character from the cartoon strip. [5]Snoopy who plays tennis and ice hockey has many human traits. [6]Charlie Brown suffers a lot because of what Lucy a neighbor does to him. [7]Lucy in turn suffers because Schroeder a boy who devotes himself to playing Beethoven on a small piano never returns her attention. [8]Charlie Brown's sister Sally is a more recent addition to the strip. [9]Many sports-minded readers of the strip enjoy Peppermint Patty a top athlete but a sleepy student. [10]Snoopy's frequent companion Woodstock is a tiny bird who types and takes dictation. [11]Linus the favorite of many "Peanuts" readers always carries a security blanket as he waits for the "Great Pumpkin" on Halloween.

[12]"Peanuts" cartoons written originally for a United States audience have been translated into many languages and distributed internationally. [13]Charlie Brown and his dog Snoopy are probably as well known as the President of the United States. [14]The greatest tribute to the popularity of "Peanuts" and Schulz's success as a cartoonist probably came when the U.S. spaceships which went to the moon were named Snoopy and Charlie Brown.

EXERCISE 2-C   *Insert commas, dashes, or parentheses where necessary in the passage below.*

HOMECOMING

[1]Homecoming with its parades, queens, and ballgames is a big event on college campuses. [2]Most homecoming weeks are held in the fall the traditional good-will season. [3]The alumni students of bygone years speak nostalgically of the good old days. [4]Sports fans who turn out in large numbers to help celebrate are especially enthusiastic at the football game. [5]The football players heroes if they win the game villains if they don't try their hardest to beat the other team their most bitter rivals. [6]The queen who reigns over the activities is usually elected by the student body. [7]Her attendants all of whom were finalists in the queen contest are also feted. [8]Schools try hard to impress visitors who may later make large financial contributions to the institution. [9]After the week is over academics which take a back seat during Homecoming become primary once again.

EXERCISE 2.1-A   *Supply additional information for each of the sentences below. Rewrite the sentences in paragraph form, placing the new information in the space provided. If the information you add is essential to the identity of the preceding noun, do not set it off with commas, dashes, or parentheses. If, on the other hand, the new information is not necessary to identify the preceding noun, set it off with the appropriate punctuation.*

CONTINENTS

1. The world's continents _____ are very different.

2. Africa _____ has an area of nearly twelve million square miles and has about 800 million people.

3. Asia _____ has approximately three billion people in its seventeen and one-half million square miles.

4. Antarctica _____ has no permanent human population on its five and one-half million square miles of land.

5. Europe _____ has around 500 million people but less than four million square miles of land.

6. Australia _____ has a population of only about seventeen million and an area of nearly three million square miles.

7. North America _____ has a population approaching 400 million and an area of 9.4 million square miles.

8. South America _____ has almost 400 million people and an area of 6,880,000 square miles.

9. Sometimes considered a continent, Oceania _____ has a population of a little over nine million and an area of over three hundred thousand square miles scattered among 25,000 islands.

EXERCISE 2.1-B   *Supply additional information for each of the sentences below. Rewrite the sentences in paragraph form, placing the new information in the space provided. If the information you add is essential to the identity of the preceding noun, do not set it off with commas, dashes, or parentheses. If, on the other hand, the new information is not necessary to identify the preceding noun, set it off with the appropriate punctuation.*

THE SOLAR SYSTEM

1. The planets of our solar system revolve around the sun _____.

2. Mercury _____ is the closest planet to the sun.

3. Venus _____ is Earth's closest neighbor.

4. We, of course, live on the Earth _____.

5. For many years earthlings have dreamed of traveling to Mars _____.

6. Jupiter _____ has twelve moons.

7. Saturn _____ is the second largest planet.

8. After Saturn comes Uranus _____.

9. Neptune _____ takes 165 earth years to revolve around the sun.

10. The ninth planet is Pluto _____.

EXERCISE 2.1-C   *Supply additional information for each of the sentences below. Rewrite the sentences in paragraph form, placing the new information in the space provided. If the information you add is essential to the identity of the preceding noun, do not set it off with commas, dashes, or parentheses. If, on the other hand, the new information is not necessary to identify the preceding noun, set it off with the appropriate punctuation.*

INVENTORS

1. Through the efforts of inventors ――――――――――― our lives have been made more productive.

2. Johann Gutenberg ――――――――――― is believed to have been the first European to print with movable type.

3. Benjamin Franklin ――――――――――― is responsible for bifocal glasses, the lightning rod, and the stove which bears his name.

4. Samuel B. Morse ――――――――――― was responsible for telegraphy, including the code of dots and dashes.

5. Alfred Nobel ――――――――――― invented dynamite.

6. Alexander Graham Bell ――――――――――― conceived the idea of transmitting speech by electricity and gave us the telephone.

7. Thomas Alva Edison ――――――――――― invented such things as wax paper, the mimeograph, the phonograph, storage batteries, and 1,089 other things.

8. Guglielmo Marconi ――――――――――― developed the wireless telegraph, the forerunner of today's radios.

9. Orville and Wilbur Wright ――――――――――― made the first flight in a power driven airplane.

10. Robert H. Goddard ――――――――――― completed and successfully fired the world's first liquid fuel rocket.

EXERCISE 2.2-A   *Write at least twenty related sentences about **modes of travel**. Then add essential or nonessential information to at least ten of your sentences.*

EXERCISE 2.2-B   *Write at least twenty related sentences about **war** or **wars**. Then add essential or nonessential information to at least ten of your sentences.*

EXERCISE 2.2-C   *Write at least twenty related sentences about **works of art**. Then add essential or nonessential information to at least ten of your sentences.*

15

Transition Words and Variety in Writing

This chapter will help you relate sentences to each other appropriately—even though they are not combined—and avoid or correct mistakes like these:

- First Cindy came here, then she went to Ruth's house.
- In my country we have a lot of ways to show respect. <u>However</u>, I'll write about them.
- Sometimes our parents tell us what to do, but we don't agree with it, <u>however</u>, we have to do it.
- In addition <u>of</u> the English language, Brenda would like to study French.
- <u>Literally</u>, for people to argue with each other is natural.
- They had not received my application papers. <u>Nevertheless</u>, they could not process them.
- I like Chinese food, <u>as a matter of fact</u>, I love it.

1. Transition Words

1.1 Sentences are seldom used in isolation. In writing, related sentences are usually grouped together in paragraphs.

Relationships between sentences within paragraphs are often shown by transition words and phrases. These **do not connect sentences**—they are part of one sentence and indicate its relationship to the preceding sentence or sentences.

Transition words function like signs on a highway. They let you know what is coming, so you can be prepared for it.

1.2 A number of different transition words or phrases may be used. The choice depends on the relationships between the sentences.

In the list below, the more common transition words and phrases are grouped according to their general meaning. Nevertheless, many have specific meanings. In other words, all the transition words or phrases within a category do not have exactly the same meaning and they cannot always be freely substituted for one another.

For example, *on the contrary* and *otherwise* both express the same general idea of difference, but *on the contrary* serves to emphasize the contrast, while *otherwise* provides a warning of unfavorable consequences.

Similarly, *by the way* and *likewise* are both used to introduce additional information, but *by the way* is used with information that is loosely (incidentally) connected to the preceding idea, while *likewise* introduces similar, parallel information.

Difference, Contrast, or Concession	Reason or Result	Time or Sequence
but	accordingly	earlier
conversely	as a consequence	finally
however*	as a result	first, second, etc.
instead*	consequently*	in the first place
nevertheless*	for this (that) reason	later
on the contrary*	hence	meanwhile
on the other hand*	therefore*	next
otherwise	thus	now
still		then
yet		

Example or Illustration	Emphasis or Clarification	Additional Information
as a matter of fact* for example for instance in fact* namely that is	after all anyway at any rate at least indeed* in fact* in other words* of course* to be sure*	also by the way* furthermore in addition incidentally* likewise moreover

*May be placed at any junction of sentence units (see section 1.4 below).

1.3   Some of these transition expressions may be used for more than one purpose:

> Tahiti has beautiful, tropical scenery. Incidentally, it also has a lot of mosquitoes.

In this case, *incidentally* introduces **additional** information which is in **contrast** with the pleasant tone of the first sentence.

1.4   Generally, transition words or phrases are set off by commas and are placed at the **beginning** of a sentence. However, some of them (those marked by an asterisk in the list above) may be placed **at any junction** of sentence units—between a front shifter and a subject, between a subject and a predicate, and between the predicate and an end shifter. Within the predicate they may also be placed between the first aux-word and the following verb (or timeless aux-word). For instance, in the following examples, the second sentence in each pair can be written in several ways, with the transition word in different locations.

> The platypus, which lives in Tasmania and Australia, lays eggs.
> *However,* it is classified as a mammal because it has mammary glands.
> OR
> It, *however,* is classified as a mammal because it has mammary glands.
> OR
> It is, *however,* classified as a mammal because it has mammary glands.
> OR
> It is classified as a mammal, *however,* because it has mammary glands.

> The platypus belongs to a very small group of primitive mammals.
> *As a matter of fact,* the spiny anteater is the only other animal in the group.
> OR
> The spiny anteater, *as a matter of fact,* is the only other animal in the group.
> OR
> The spiny anteater is, *as a matter of fact,* the only other animal in the group.

EXERCISE 1-A   *Underline and label each of the transition words in the passage below according to the relationship between sentences (i.e., contrast, time, reason, etc.) which it shows.*

THE GUINNESS BOOK OF WORLD RECORDS

[1]The first *Guinness Book of World Records* appeared in 1956. [2]At that time, the McWhirter brothers, its authors, were not inundated by people's requests to get their names in the book. [3]The brothers, consequently, did considerable research to find the facts to include in their book. [4]Today status seekers even invent new items or events to get their names into this book. [5]Still, it is not easy to get into the *Guinness Book of Records*. [6]It can be done, however. [7]In the first place, one must have actual proof of his or her record. [8]Furthermore, the word of a friend or relative is not considered proof. [9]Moreover, the record must be legal and moral. [10]In fact, it is easier to get in this record book by beating an established record than by creating a new category or event. [11]Also, it helps to have the record reported in the news media. [12]Of course, affidavits signed by witnesses must accompany your request when you finally write for your claim to fame. [13]That is, if you manage to break an existing record.

EXERCISE 1-B   *Underline and label each of the transition words in the passage below according to the relationship between sentences (i.e., contrast, time, reason, etc.) which it shows.*

DOLPHINS

[1]With their shiny, graceful, gray bodies, dolphins appear to be large fish. [2]Nevertheless, they are really warm-blooded mammals. [3]As a result, although they can dive as deep as a thousand feet and stay underwater for up to fifteen minutes at a time, dolphins, like whales, must surface to breathe air through a blowhole on top of their heads.

[4]Dolphins are social animals and love company. [5]Many of them, in fact, even enjoy being around humans. [6]It is not uncommon to hear of dolphins giving rides through the water to humans.

[7]In addition to being playful, dolphins are helpful to men. [8]For example, as early as 400 B.C. the Greek poet Arion was saved from drowning by a dolphin. [9]From then until now, dolphins have been helping swimmers who are in trouble. [10]Swimmers, however, are not the only humans they help. [11]In some parts of the world, they can be counted on to help men catch fish.

[12]Moreover, dolphins are very intelligent. [13]A dolphin's brain resembles a human brain, but it is larger. [14]Consequently, some people claim that dolphins are really smarter than humans. [15]Of course, there is no way of proving this point. [16]Brain size is not an absolute measure of intelligence. [17]Furthermore, measuring dolphins' intelligence in other ways is not possible since humans

cannot fully communicate with them. [18]Apparently, however, dolphins communicate with each other. [19]At any rate, they make whistling, clicking, and buzzing sounds that seem to be at least a form of language. [20]So far, however, humans have not been able to figure out the communication code the dolphins use. [21]Thus, no one really knows what they are thinking. [22]If we could communicate with dolphins, perhaps they could teach us to be as happy as they seem to be. [23]At least that is what some people think.

EXERCISE 1-C   *Underline and label each of the transition words in the passage below according to the relationship between sentences (i.e., contrast, time, reason, etc.) which it shows.*

PUZZLES

[1]Occasionally, people do not enjoy active sports. [2]They do, however, like mental competition. [3]In these cases, puzzles are one pastime in which people can compete without an active opponent. [4]In the first place, anyone who has had a pleasant experience in solving pencil and paper games is more apt to try the sport again. [5]Furthermore, he may even be interested in trying more difficult games. [6]On the other hand, one who has not had success may possibly turn to another type of puzzle or may give up the sport altogether. [7]For years, puzzle magazines have been listing their crossword puzzles as easy, medium, or difficult. [8]As a result, a person who has not tried a crossword puzzle before may begin with an easy one and have success. [9]He may then try a harder puzzle and solve it. [10]Thus it is possible to become proficient in a very short time without becoming frustrated. [11]Soon the puzzle fan will be able to solve more challenging puzzles. [12]Eventually, even a puzzle labeled *challenger* will not stop him.

EXERCISE 1.1-A   *Supply appropriate transition words in the numbered blanks. Make sure that the transition words you choose show the proper relationships between sentences.*

AMERICAN INDIANS

It is often thought that the American Indians were all savages.

_____, it is easy to get this idea from watching movies and
　　　　　1

television programs. Examining historical evidence, _____,
　　　　　　　　　　　　　　　　　　　　　　2

reveals a quite different picture. There were many different Indian tribes and

types of Indians, and, _____, different Indians behaved in
　　　　　　　　　　　3

different ways.

_____, some Indian tribes seemed to be more civilized
   <u>4</u>

than the Europeans who came to America from across the Atlantic.

_____, there were other Indians whose civilizations were very
   <u>5</u>

primitive.

A number of famous Indian tribes, _____, were very warlike.
                                        <u>6</u>

Many other tribes, _____, lived very peacefully and used
                        <u>7</u>

weapons only for hunting food. Still others did not use weapons at all but were

completely agricultural.

_____, anyone who makes sweeping generalizations about
   <u>8</u>

American Indians is making a big mistake.

EXERCISE 1.1-B   *Supply appropriate transition words in the numbered blanks. Make sure that the
transition words you choose show the proper relationships between sentences.*

MEN AND FLIGHT

Many Americans believe that the Wright Brothers were the first men to fly.

_____, men had ascended high into the sky over one hundred
   <u>1</u>

years before the Wright Brothers made their historic first flight.

In 1783, the first successful hydrogen-filled balloon carried men aloft to an

altitude of 3,000 feet for 45 minutes. _____, French soldiers used
                                             <u>2</u>

balloons for military purposes. _____, in 1860, the world's first
                                       <u>3</u>

successful aerial photographs were made from a balloon flying over Boston.

_____, gas-filled balloons were used for observation of the
   <u>4</u>

enemy during the U.S. Civil War. _____, hot air balloons were
                                        <u>5</u>

developed.

All of these airships, _____, flew because they were "lighter
                            <u>6</u>

than air." _____, men, like the Wright Brothers, would
                <u>7</u>

develop machines that would fly even though they were heavier than air. This

development, _____, would have to wait until the necessary
                  <u>8</u>

power sources were available. _____, in the years before the
                                     <u>9</u>

twentieth century, balloons offered men the only means of flight.

EXERCISE 1.1-C   *Supply appropriate transition words in the numbered blanks. Make sure that the transition words you choose show the proper relationships between sentences.*

INDIAN CIVILIZATIONS

Some of the most advanced civilizations in the world developed in pre-Columbian South and Central America. _____, early Spanish

1
explorers expected to find a civilization inferior to the one they had left behind in Europe. What they found in the new world, _____, surprised

2
them. Even those who had seen the greatest cities of Europe at that time marveled at the grandeur of some of the new world cities.

Tenochtitlán (Mexico City today), the capital of the Aztec empire, surpassed all the others. _____, the Spanish conquistadores took

3
advantage of the facilities Tenochtitlán offered. _____, when

4
Cortez, the conqueror of Mexico, was wounded, he agreed to be treated by an Indian doctor—he saw no need to send for a European physician.

_____, he reported that the medical care he had received was

5
more than adequate by European standards.

_____, the Mayan civilization, which preceded

6
the Aztec culture, was even more highly developed in many ways.

_____, by the time the Spanish arrived its glory had ceased to

7
exist. _____, no one really knows why the Mayan civilization

8
declined.

2. Variety in Writing

As explained in Chapter 12, section 3, good writing demands variety in sentence length and combining/transforming methods. Some simple sentences should remain as they are while others should be combined by using different methods. When writing, do not overuse any one sentence combining or transforming method.

EXERCISE 2-A   *Rewrite the sentences below into a paragraph (or paragraphs). Vary the length of your sentences and use a variety of transforming/combining methods. Where appropriate, use transition words.*

EINSTEIN

Albert Einstein was born on March 14, 1879.

Young Albert was born in Ulm, Germany.

Albert Einstein's father was a small merchant and manufacturer.

Young Albert went to elementary school in Munich, Germany.

Later he went to school in Switzerland.

He was a physicist.

He advanced the theory of general relativity.

He is known throughout the world today.

He was the most eminent scientist of this century.

Some claim he was the greatest scientist of all time.

His theories were very advanced.

He first proposed the theory that mass and energy are equivalent and interchangeable.

His astonishing theory of relativity has been verified by modern scientists.

The greatest proof of his theories has come since his death.

He opened the door to nuclear fission.

He received the Nobel Prize in 1921.

He disliked publicity and honors.

He helped form the Hebrew University.

The Hebrew University is in Jerusalem.

He spent his last twenty-two years at the Institute for Advanced Study.

The Institute for Advanced Study is in Princeton, New Jersey.

Albert Einstein died April 18, 1955.

EXERCISE 2-B   *Rewrite the sentences below into a paragraph (or paragraphs). Vary the length of your sentences and use a variety of transforming/combining methods. Where appropriate, use transition words.*

PRIMATES

Monkeys belong to the primate family.

Apes belong to the primate family.

The primate family is one of the major groups of mammals.

Primates nurse their young with milk.

The word "primate" comes from the Latin word *primus*.

Primus means "first."

Scientists classify men as primates.

Most primates live in tropical places.

Men live in almost all regions of the world.

Men live in almost all climates of the world.

A few primates live on the ground.

Most primates spend their time in trees.

Primates have good eyes.

Primates have grasping hands.

Primates have grasping feet.

Primates' bodies are well suited to life in the trees.

Primates have large eyes.

Primates' eyes look straight forward.

Higher primates can focus both eyes on the same object.

This ability helps them judge distances.

Some primates also see colors.

Many other mammals have claws.

Primates have flat nails on their fingers.

Primates have flat nails on their toes.

The nails help support enlarged pads.

The pads are on the ends of their fingers.

The pads are on the ends of their toes.

The pads are sensitive to touch.

The pads have nonskid ridges.

Most primates have large brains.

Primates are among the most intelligent of mammals.

Primates do not depend much on their sense of smell.

One part of their brain is relatively small.

This part is related to the sense of smell.

Primates have fewer young than most mammals.

A mother bears only one or two young at a time.

The young primates stay with their mothers for a longer period of time.

The longer period with their mothers allows the young primates to learn more.

Young primates learn from their mothers.

Young primates learn from the group they live in.

EXERCISE 2-C   *Rewrite the sentences below into a paragraph (or paragraphs). Vary the length of your sentences and use a variety of transforming/combining methods. Where appropriate, use transition words.*

CHESS

Chess is the most popular game in the world.

The kings lead the chess armies.

The kings face all kinds of dangerous situations.

Castles attack them.

Bishops attack them.

Knights attack them.

The knights are on horseback.

The king is trapped.

The king must surrender to the other army.

The game is over.

Every new game of chess is a different battle.

The two players are the generals.

The generals plan the battle.

Chess originated in India and Persia.

Chess originated more than 1300 years ago.

Chess is a "royal" game.

Chess provides challenge for adults.

Chess provides challenge for children.

Chess provides excitement for adults.

Chess provides excitement for children.

The word "chess" comes from a Persian word.

The Persian word is *shah*.

Shah means king.

"Checkmate" comes from an Arabic phrase.

The Arabic phrase is *shah mat*.

Shah mat means "the king is dead."

Chess is very popular in some countries.

Chess champions in these countries are famous.

Sports heroes are famous in other countries.

Chess is played by people all over the world.

EXERCISE 2.1-A   *Selecting information from the facts given below, write correct basic sentences. Then combine your sentences appropriately and write them in paragraph form. The result will be a short descriptive (or comparative) essay.*

SCOUTING IN THE UNITED STATES

Members:

Boy Scouts
Cub Scouts: boys 8–11 years old
Boy Scouts: boys 12–13 years old
Varsity Scouts: boys 14–15 years old
Explorer Scouts: boys 16–18 years old

Girl Scouts
Brownies: girls 7–8 years old
Junior Girl Scouts: girls 9–11 years old
Cadette Girl Scouts: girls 12–14 years old
Senior Girl Scouts: girls 14–17 years old

Beginnings:

Boy Scouts
Founded by Lord Baden-Powell, England, 1908
Incorporated in the United States, 1910
National charter granted by U.S. Congress, 1916

Girl Scouts
Founded by Mrs. Juliette Gordon Low, Savannah, Georgia, 1912

Ranks:
Cub Scouts—bobcat, wolf, bear, and webelos
Boy Scouts—tenderfoot, second-class, first-class, star, life, and eagle

Emphases:
Threefold development—mental, moral, and physical

Stresses:

Boy Scouts
Outdoor knowledge and skills, training in citizenship, manual arts, wood and camp craft, lifesaving, first aid, sports and games

Girl Scouts
Agriculture, arts and crafts, community life, health and safety, homemaking, international friendship, nature, sports and games

Publications:
Boy Scouts—*Boy's Life*
Girl Scouts—*American Girl*

EXERCISE 2.1-B   *Selecting information from the facts given below, write correct basic sentences. Then combine your sentences appropriately and write them in paragraph form. The result will be a short descriptive essay.*

REPUBLIC OF IRELAND

Name: Republic of Ireland, *Éire* (in Gaelic)
Earlier names: Irish Free State (1922–1937) and Éire (1937–1949)
Capital: Dublin
Major cities: Dublin, Cork, Limerick, Galway, Waterford
Location: Island in eastern North Atlantic Ocean, near England
Area: 27,136 square miles
Highest point: Carrantuohill (3,414 feet above sea level)
Lowest point: coast (sea level)
Languages: Gaelic (Irish) and English
Religion: 94% Roman Catholic, Episcopalian 5%
Government: Republic
Head of State: President
Head of Government: Prime Minister
International Cooperation: United Nations (UN), Organization for Economic Co-Operation and Development (OECD), Council of Europe
National Anthem: *Amhran na Oh Fiann* ("The Soldier's Song")
Economy:
    Agriculture—livestock, dairy products, wheat, barley, potatoes, turnips, sugar beets, and oats
    Industries and products—bread and biscuit making, brewing, textile milling, whiskey distilling, metal products, and paper
    Chief exports—live animals, foodstuffs, beverages, processed tobacco, textiles, and manufactured goods
    Chief imports—machinery and electrical goods, vehicles, iron and steel, coal and petroleum products
Monetary unit: Irish pound

EXERCISE 2.1-C   *Selecting information from the facts given below, write correct basic sentences. Then combine your sentences appropriately and write them in paragraph form. The result will be a short descriptive essay.*

SHAKESPEARE

Name: William Shakespeare
Born: 1564, Stratford-on-Avon, England
Died: 1616, Stratford-on-Avon, England (age: 52)

Father: prosperous businessman and town mayor
Education: Latin grammar school
Married: 1582, to Anne Hathaway, a neighboring farm girl 8 years his senior
Children: three—Susanna, Hamnet, and Judith
Stage life:
    1592, successful actor in London
    1592–1594, London theaters closed because of plague, Shakespeare writes
      poetry
    1594, joins Chamberlain's Men, company of actors
    1599, Chamberlain's Men build Globe theater
    1603, King James comes to throne, Chamberlain's Men become the King's Men
    1610, Shakespeare retires from stage
Major types of plays and examples of each:

Comedies	Histories	Tragedies	Romances
The Comedy of Errors	*Henry VI* (3 parts)	*Romeo and Juliet*	*The Winter's Tale*
The Taming of the Shrew	*Richard II*	*Julius Caesar*	*The Tempest*
Much Ado about Nothing	*Richard III*	*Hamlet*	*Cymbeline*
As You Like It	*Henry IV* (2 parts)	*Othello*	*Pericles, Prince of Tyre*
	Henry V	*Macbeth*	
	Henry VIII	*Antony and Cleopatra*	

Total number of plays written: 36

EXERCISE 2.2-A   *Selecting information from the facts given below, write correct basic sentences. Then combine your sentences appropriately and write them in paragraph form. The result will be a short process (history) essay.*

MAJOR EARTHQUAKES

Date	Place	Deaths	Magnitude*
526 May 20	Syria, Antioch	250,000	N.A.
1290 Sept. 27	China, Chihli	100,000	N.A.
1556 Jan. 24	China, Shaanxi	830,000	N.A.
1730 Dec. 30	Japan, Hokkaido	137,000	N.A.
1737 Oct. 11	India, Calcutta	300,000	N.A.
1908 Dec. 28	Italy, Messina	83,000	7.5**
1920 Dec. 16	China, Gansu	100,000	8.6
1923 Sept. 1	Japan, Tokyo	99,330	8.3
1927 May 22	China, Nan-Shan	200,000	8.3
1970 May 31	Northern Peru	66,794	7.7
1976 Feb. 4	Guatemala	22,778	7.5
1976 July 23	China, Tangshan	655,235	8.2
1978 Sept. 16	Northeast Iran	25,000	7.7
1979 Sept. 12	Indonesia	100	8.1
1985 Sept. 19, 21	Mexico City	4,200+	8.1
1988 Dec. 7	Northwest Armenia	55,000+	6.8
1989 Oct. 17	San Francisco Bay Area	62	6.9
1990 June 21	Northwest Iran	40,000+	7.7

*Magnitude of earthquakes is measured on the Richter scale. Each higher number represents a tenfold increase in energy measured in ground motion. N.A. indicates that information on the magnitude is not available.

**Magnitude has been estimated from earthquake intensity.

EXERCISE 2.2-B   *Selecting information from the facts given below, write correct basic sentences. Then combine your sentences appropriately and write them in paragraph form. The result will be a short process (history) essay.*

MAN'S JOURNEY TO THE MOON

Date	Crew	Mission Name	Orbits	Duration	Remarks
4/12/61	Gagarin	Vostok 1	1	1h48m	First manned orbital flight
5/5/61	Shepard	Mercury-Redstone 3	*	15m22s	First American in space
8/6–7/61	Titov	Vostok 2	16	25h18m	First space flight of more than 24 hours
2/20/62	Glenn	Mercury-Atlas 6	3	4h55m23s	First American in orbit
8/11–15/62	Nikolayev	Vostok 3	64	94h22m	Vostok 3 and 4 made first group flight
8/12–15/62	Popovich	Vostok 4	48	70h57m	Came within 32 miles of Vostok 3
6/16–19/63	Tereshkova	Vostok 6	58	70h50m	First woman in space
10/12/64	Komarov, Feoktistov, & Yegorov	Voskhod 1	16	24h17m	First 3-man orbital flight; first without space suits
3/13/65	Belyayev & Leonov	Voskhod 2	17	26h02m	Leonov made first "space walk" (10 min.)
3/23/65	Grissom & Young	Gemini-Titan 3	3	4h53m00s	First manned spacecraft to change its orbital path
12/15–16/65	Schirra & Stafford	Gemini-Titan 6-A	16	25h51m24s	Completed world's first space rendezvous with Gemini 7
12/21–27/68	Borman, Lovell, & Anders	Apollo-Saturn 8	10**	147h00m42s	First flight to moon; views of lunar surface televised to earth
3/3–13/69	McDivitt, Scott, & Schweickart	Apollo-Saturn 9	151	241h00m54s	First manned flight of lunar module
5/13–26/69	Stafford, Cernan, & Young	Apollo-Saturn 10	31**	192h03m23s	First lunar module orbit of moon
7/16–24/69	Armstrong, Aldrin, & Collins	Apollo-Saturn 11	30**	195h18m35s	First lunar landing made by Armstrong & Aldrin; collected soil, rock samples; lunar stay time 21h36m21s

*suborbital
**moon orbits

EXERCISE 2.2-C   *Selecting information from the facts given below, write correct basic sentences. Then combine your sentences appropriately and write them in paragraph form. The result will be a short process (history) essay.*

NOTABLE HEAVYWEIGHT BOXING CHAMPIONSHIP BOUTS

Year	Winner	Loser	Place	Notes
1889	John L. Sullivan	Jake Kilrain	Richburg, Miss.	Last bare knuckles championship bout.
1908	Jack Johnson	Tommy Burns	Sydney, Australia	Knock out. Police halted the contest.
1915	Jess Willard	Jack Johnson	Havana, Cuba	Knock out.
1919	Jack Dempsey	Jess Willard	Toledo, Ohio	Knock out.
1926	Gene Tunney	Jack Dempsey	Philadelphia	Tunney retired as champ in 1928.
1937	Joe Louis	James Braddock	Chicago	Knockout. Louis retired as champ in 1949.
1952	Rocky Marciano	Joe Walcott	Philadelphia	Knock out. Marciano returned undefeated in 1956.

(continued)

Year	Winner	Loser	Place	Notes
1956	Floyd Patterson	Archie Moore	Chicago	Knock out.
1959	Ingemar Johansson	Floyd Patterson	New York	Knock out.
1960	Floyd Patterson	Ingemar Johansson	New York	First heavyweight in boxing history to regain title.
1962	Sonny Liston	Floyd Patterson	Chicago	Knock out.
1964	Cassius Clay	Sonny Liston	Miami Beach	Clay later changed name to Muhammad Ali. Refused to serve in military and stripped of title in 1967.
1971	Joe Frazier	Cassius Clay	New York	
1973	George Foreman	Joe Frazier	Kingston, Jamaica	
1974	Muhammad Ali	George Foreman	Zaire	Knock out. Ali regained title.
1978	Leon Spinks	Muhammad Ali	Las Vegas	
1978	Muhammad Ali	Leon Spinks	New Orleans	Ali regained title second time, retired in 1979.
1985	Michael Spinks	Larry Holmes	Las Vegas	Spinks gained IBF title only.
1987	Mike Tyson	James Smith	Las Vegas	Tyson gained WBA title only.
1990	"Buster" Douglas	Mike Tyson	Tokyo	Knock out. Douglas gained WBA, WBC, & IBF titles.

EXERCISE 2.3-A

Selecting information from the facts given below, write correct basic sentences. Then combine your sentences appropriately and write them in paragraph form. The result will be a short comparison/contrast essay.

FAMOUS PRESIDENTS OF THE UNITED STATES

Name	Born	State	Political Party	Education	In Office
John F. Kennedy	1917	Massachusetts	Democratic	B.S. from Harvard	1961–1963
Franklin D. Roosevelt	1882	New York	Democratic	Columbia Law School	1933–1945
Theodore Roosevelt	1858	New York	Republican	Harvard & Columbia	1901–1909
Woodrow Wilson	1856	Virginia	Democratic	Princeton & John Hopkins	1913–1921
Abraham Lincoln	1809	Kentucky	Republican	Mostly self-educated	1861–1865
Thomas Jefferson	1743	Virginia	Democratic-Republican	College of William & Mary	1801–1808
George Washington	1732	Virginia	—	Mathematics & surveying	1789–1796

EXERCISE 2.3-B

Selecting information from the facts given below, write correct basic sentences. Then combine your sentences appropriately and write them in paragraph form. The result will be a short comparison/contrast essay.

OCEANS AND SEAS

Name	Area*	Average Depth**	Deepest Point	Depth**
Pacific Ocean	64,186,300	13,739	Mariana Trench	36,198
Atlantic Ocean	33,420,000	12,257	Puerto Rico Trench	28,374
Indian Ocean	28,350,500	12,704	Java Trench	25,344
Arctic Ocean	5,105,700	4,362	Eurasia Basin	17,880
South China Sea	1,148,500	4,802	—	
Caribbean Sea	971,400	8,448	—	
Mediterranean Sea	969,100	4,926	Ionian Basin	16,896
Bering Sea	873,000	4,893	—	
Gulf of Mexico	582,100	5,297	—	
Sea of Japan	391,100	5,468	—	

*Areas are given in square miles

**Depths are given in feet

EXERCISE 2.3-C   *Selecting information from the facts given below, write correct basic sentences. Then combine your sentences appropriately and write them in paragraph form. The result will be a short comparison/contrast essay.*

AVERAGE TEMPERATURES* AROUND THE WORLD

Place	January	April	July	October
Copenhagen, Demark	32	42	62	48
Paris, France	37	50	66	52
Rome, Italy	44	58	77	62
Cairo, Egypt	56	70	83	75
Cape Town, South Africa	70	63	55	62
Hong Kong	60	71	83	77
Tokyo, Japan	39	55	76	62
Bangkok, Thailand	80	87	84	83
Sydney, Australia	72	61	53	64
Rio de Janeiro, Brazil	78	77	69	72
Buenos Aires, Argentina	74	63	50	60
Mexico City, Mexico	54	65	64	60

*All temperatures given in Fahrenheit.

A

Verbs That May Be Followed by Noun Phrases

Followed by *-ing* Forms Only

admit
allow
appreciate
avoid
can't help
consider
deny
enjoy
escape
finish
get through
imagine
insist on
keep on
make
mind
miss
plan on
postpone
practice
resent
resist
stop
study
suggest

Followed by *to* + Base Form Only

agree
appear
ask
beg
care
decide
deserve
endeavor
expect
forget
hope
intend
learn
mean
need
plan
promise
want
wish

Followed by Either Form

afford
attempt
begin
continue
go
like
prefer
remember
start
stop
try

B

Exercice Titles

CHAPTER EIGHT

2-A   A Dangerous Voyage
2-B   Strange Sights
2-C   Records
4-A   Athletics
4-B   An Essay
4-C   A Garden
5-A   Employers and Employees
5-B   The Theater
5-C   Elections
6-A   Writing English
6-B   Football Fever
6-C   An Unfamiliar Country
7-A   The Continents of the World–Areas and
       Populations Over the Years
7-B   Information on the Planets
7-C   Ten Major Lakes of the World
9-A   Water
9-B   Police Work
9-C   Bad Deal at the Trading Post
11-A Domestic Difficulties
11-B A Good Movie
11-C An Exciting Football Game
12-A Sports on TV
12-B The Olympic Games
12-C My Secret Talent

CHAPTER NINE

1-A   Eating Styles
1-B   A Western
1-C   Houses
2-A   The Saber-Tooth Tiger
2-B   Champion Animals
2-C   Sound

2.1-A Living Things
2.1-B Rope
2.1-C A New Knot
3-A   Animal Eyes
3-B   Fish Bait
3-C   The Armadillo
3.1-A Carving
3.1-B Pigs: Intelligence and Courage
3.1-C Spider Webs

CHAPTER TEN

1-A   Tidal Energy
1-B   Camouflage
1-C   Hazardous Habits
2-A   A Football Game
2-B   A Party
2-C   A Game-Winning Play
2.1-A Air Mail
2.1-B Survival in the Desert
2.1-C Soccer Fever
3-A   Baseballs
3-B   Teachers and Tests
3-C   Halloween

CHAPTER ELEVEN

1-A   The Great Train Robbery
1-B   The Taj Mahal
1-C   Catalog Business
3-A   Carbohydrates
3-B   A Dangerous Drive
3-C   Norman Rockwell
4-A   The Nobel Prize
4-B   The Colonization of Space
4-C   Language Acquisition by Apes

CHAPTER TWELVE

1-A   Cookbook Recipes
1-B   Superstitions
1-C   Comic Books
1.1-A Television Programs
1.1-B Earthquakes
1.1-C Arable Land
2-A   Color
2-B   The Horseshoe Crab
2-C   Body Language
2.1-A Endangered Species
2.1-B From Typewriter to Word Processor
2.1-C Inventions and Inventors
3-A   The Bastille
3-B   Perception
3-C   Right-Side-Upness

CHAPTER THIRTEEN

1-A   Self-Education
1-B   Competition: Mental vs. Physical
1-C   Polynesian Navigators
2-A   Identification Tags
2-B   Twin Language
2-C   The Dead Sea Scrolls
3-A   A Strange Encounter
3-B   Strange Records
3-C   A Confession
4-A   Returning Home
4-B   An Invitation to the Circus
4-C   Lost in the Country
5-A   Leisure Time Activities
5-B   My Vocation
5-C   A New Skill
6-A   City vs. Country Life
6-B   Music
6-C   Nutrition

7-A   Terry's Ambition
7-B   Sister Knows Best
7-C   A Family Garden

CHAPTER FOURTEEN

1-A   Australian Animals
1-B   Illegal Aliens
1-C   Refugees
2-A   Language
2-B   "Peanuts"
2-C   Homecoming
2.1-A Continents
2.1-B The Solar System
2.1-C Inventors

CHAPTER FIFTEEN

1-A   The Guiness Book of World Records
1-B   Dolphins
1-C   Puzzles
1.1-A American Indians
1.1-B Men and Flight
1.1-C Indian Civilizations
2-A   Einstein
2-B   Primates
2-C   Chess
2.1-A Scouting in the United States
2.1-B Republic of Ireland
2.1-C Shakespeare
2.2-A Major Earthquakes
2.2-B Man's Journey to the Moon
2.2-C Notable Heavyweight Boxing Championship
      Bouts
2.3-A Famous Presidents of the United States
2.3-B Oceans and Seas
2.3-C Average Temperatures Around the World